RESURGENCE

Engaging With Indigenous Narratives and
Cultural Expressions In and Beyond the Classroom

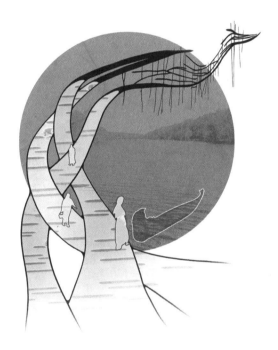

Edited by Christine M'Lot and Katya Adamov Ferguson

PORTAGE &
MAIN PRESS

Portage & Main Press gratefully acknowledges the financial support of
the Province of Manitoba through the Department of Sport, Culture and Heritage
and the Manitoba Book Publishing Tax Credit, and the Government of
Canada through the Canada Book Fund (CBF) for our publishing activities.

Printed and bound in Canada by Friesens
Design by Jennifer Lum
Cover art by Reanna Merasty

Library and Archives Canada Cataloguing in Publication

Title: Resurgence : engaging with Indigenous narratives and cultural expressions
in and beyond the classroom / edited by Christine M'Lot and Katya Ferguson.
Other titles: Resurgence (2022) | Connecting Indigenous narratives and
cultural expressions with the K-12 classroom
Names: M'Lot, Christine (Educator), editor. | Ferguson, Katya, editor.
Description: Series statement: Footbridge series ; 1 | Includes bibliographical references.
Identifiers: Canadiana (print) 20210207159 | Canadiana (ebook) 2021021161X
ISBN 9781774920008 (softcover) | ISBN 9781774920022 (PDF) | ISBN 9781774920015 (EPUB)
Subjects: LCSH: Culturally relevant pedagogy—Canada.
CSH: Canadian literature (English)— | Indigenous authors—Study and teaching.
Classification: LCC PS8033.5 .R47 2022 | DDC C810.9/897071071—dc23

25 24 23 22   1 2 3 4 5

	TREES	WATER	ENERGY	SOLID WASTE	GREENHOUSE GASES
	31	2,500	13	100	13,200
	FULLY GROWN	GALLONS	MILLION BTUs	POUNDS	POUNDS

ENVIRONMENTAL BENEFITS STATEMENT
Portage & Main Press saved the following resources
by printing the pages of this book on chlorine free
paper made with 30% post-consumer waste.

Environmental impact estimates were made using the Environmental Paper Network
Paper Calculator 4.0. For more information visit www.papercalculator.org

PORTAGE &
MAIN PRESS
www.portageandmainpress.com
Winnipeg, Manitoba
Treaty 1 Territory and homeland of the Métis Nation

To my kookum, Vina Swain,
along with all the other children who attended
residential school. May this book be an attestation to your
power, strength, and resilience.
—C. M.

To the next generation.
May you find your powerful voice of resurgence
that lives within you.
—K. A. F.

Contents

Acknowledgments *1*

Introduction *2*
Indigenous Pedagogical Approaches *5*

How This Book Is Organized *7*
Part Overviews: Becoming Story-Ready *7*
Contributor Biographies *10*
Contributor Narratives and Expressions *10*
Educator Connections *11*
Classroom Connections *12*

PART ONE: RESISTANCE *25*

Beyond Being Silenced by Sara Florence Davidson *29*
Educator Connections *34*
Classroom Connections *36*

Poetry as a Cultural Expression: if the land could speak
and "one morning after the rain" by Rita Bouvier *41*
Educator Connections *49*
Classroom Connections *50*

Ṫseḵa Reflection and "Ṫseḵa" by Lucy Hemphill *57*
Educator Connections *59*
Classroom Connections *60*

"Holy Eucharist" and "miyo kisikaw" by Louise Bernice Halfe *65*
Educator Connections *69*
Classroom Connections *71*

PART TWO: RESILIENCE 77

"Seen in a Good Way": Reading and Writing Through
Mental Health Struggles by David A. Robertson 81
Educator Connections 85
Classroom Connections 86

Writing as a Therapeutic Medium by Wanda John-Kehewin 91
Educator Connections 95
Classroom Connections 97

Birch Bark Technology by KC Adams 101
Educator Connections 105
Classroom Connections 106

Images and Health by Lisa Boivin 113
Educator Connections 116
Classroom Connections 117

PART THREE: RESTORING 123

Stories Are Resurgence
by Charlene Bearhead and Wilson Bearhead 127
Educator Connections 129
Classroom Connections 130

Why Am I Not on Star Trek? by Sonya Ballantyne 135
Educator Connections 139
Classroom Connections 140

Indigenizing Spaces: Identity in the Built Environment
by Reanna Merasty 145
Educator Connections 152
Classroom Connections 154

Games as Resurgence by Elizabeth LaPensée 159
Educator Connections 164
Classroom Connections 167

PART FOUR: RECONNECTING *171*

"alpine mountains" and "frog whisperers" by Nicola I. Campbell *175*
Educator Connections *178*
Classroom Connections *179*

The Paths of Tradition by Russell Wallace *185*
Educator Connections *187*
Classroom Connections *189*

Making a Comeback as an Artist by Victoria McIntosh *193*
Educator Connections *197*
Classroom Connections *198*

We Are Inherently Mathematical by Christina Lavalley Ruddy *203*
Educator Connections *209*
Classroom Connections *211*

Acknowledgments

FIRST, WE'D LIKE to thank all the contributors! Without your voices, this project wouldn't have been possible. We hope we have found ways to support educators in bringing your dynamic voices into discussions while maintaining the integrity of your stories. We'd also like to thank Portage & Main Press for the powerful opportunity to learn from the contributors and each other. It's been a pleasure and an honour to work alongside everyone who had a part in the creation of this book.

We want to acknowledge that the Footbridge Series was the idea of award-winning poet and writer Garry Thomas Morse (Kwakwa̱ka̱'wakw), who introduced us to each other and invited us to join in this project. The construction of the footbridge began because of Garry's relationships and connections, and we thank him for initiating discussions with this phenomenal group of Indigenous contributors. We are grateful for his brilliant vision.

Christine: I'd also like to thank my family, partner, friends, and especially my students, for inspiring me to keep learning so that I can be better for them.

Katya: Thank you to my family and learning communities, who have been so supportive. Thank you to Indigenous Elders who, despite the horrendous history, have generously guided and made space for settler teachers who want to learn from past mistakes. Thank you to Dr. Jeannie Kerr for your mentorship in learning through wholistic engagement with Dr. Jo-ann Archibald's storywork principles.

Introduction

CHRISTINE M'LOT (she/her/hers) is an Anishinaabe educator and curriculum developer from Winnipeg, Manitoba. She has experience working with children and youth in multiple capacities, including child welfare, children's disability services, and Indigenous family programming. She currently teaches high school at the University of Winnipeg Collegiate. To learn more about Christine's projects and initiatives, visit www.christinemlot.com.

KATYA ADAMOV FERGUSON (she/her/hers) is a mother, artist, researcher, and teacher. Katya currently works as an early years support teacher in several schools in Winnipeg, Manitoba, and is passionate about teacher professional learning in the area of Indigenous education. She sees potential in the arts to create ethical spaces to mobilize complex topics with both children and adults. Katya is also a PhD student engaging in curriculum redesign and place-based inquiries, and is working on branching her arts-based research into public spaces.

As EDUCATORS, IT is our privilege and responsibility to integrate Indigenous content and learning processes into our classrooms. We—an Indigenous educator and a non-Indigenous educator—chose to write this book together to show that the work of finding ways to include Indigenous voices and perspectives in our practice is for everyone. We are committed to learning, unlearning, and relearning what it means to honour Indigenous perspectives and ways of knowing, learning, and being, and we hope you will be motivated to take action by our insights and inquiries as educators and as individuals travelling the path toward reconciliation.

We have noticed that curriculum documents often have a long way to go in terms of meaningfully integrating Indigenous content in the K–12 classroom.

Indigenous representation is often included only as an extension or add-on or is, in many cases, nowhere to be found. There is a need for educational resources led by Indigenous voices and focused on Indigenous perspectives.

At the same time, Indigenous expressions are (re)surging in communities across what is now called Canada. The word *resurgence* means to "rise to prominence." It is a fitting title for this book, which is a celebration of Indigenous voices, featuring narrative, poetic, and artistic works. For simplicity, we refer to these various narrative and cultural expressions as *texts* throughout the book. The texts shared here represent an active movement that deserves attention—a movement of contemporary Indigenous stories that are also rooted in the past.

Mi'kmaw scholar Marie Battiste describes resurgence as a revival initiated by Indigenous activism that represents "the regeneration of the dignity and cultural integrity of Indigenous peoples where success has been found in affirming and activating the holistic systems of Indigenous knowledges, engaging Elders, communities, and committed individuals."[1] In contrast to reconciliation, which has been critiqued as "for the colonizers"[2] and for failing to offer the multilayered changes needed to support Indigenous communities, resurgence signals a shift in power that gives prominence to voices of Indigenous communities.

While working on this project, we became more attuned to a sort of "curriculum of resurgence" gaining strength, power, and volume around us. As we were reading and viewing the contributors' texts, we took note of resurgence within Indigenous communities across what is now known as Canada, from Mi'kmaw fishing rights being defended in the east to Wet'suwet'en communities protecting the land and waters from pipelines in the west. The Land Back and Idle No More movements continued to strengthen. In 2021, hundreds, then thousands, of Indigenous children's bodies were uncovered

---

1   Marie Battiste, "Nourishing the Learning Spirit: Living Our Way to New Thinking," *Education Canada* 50, no. 1 (2010): 17, www.edcan.ca/wp-content/uploads/EdCan-2010-v50-n1-Battiste.pdf.

2   Andrea Landry, "This Reconciliation Is for the Colonizer," *Indigenous Motherhood*, June 13, 2017, indigenousmotherhood.wordpress.com/2017/06/13/this-reconciliation-is-for-the-colonizer/.

at former residential school sites. Indigenous communities responded with ceremonies, artistic tributes, and reminders about the unfinished Calls to Action of the Truth and Reconciliation Commission. This unearthing of tragedy led to actions such as the toppling of statues representing colonial figures in major city centres. In 2021, Canada declared a National Day for Truth and Reconciliation and appointed its first Indigenous (Inuk) governor general, Mary (Ningiukudluk) Simon. These pivotal stories of resurgence are changing society and what needs to be taught in schools.

Each text in this book is the deeply personal expression of the contributor, but together they make a statement, talking back to the many facets of coloniality. Battiste notes that the Eurocentrism of public schooling has contributed to an erosion of spirit that has created roadblocks for Indigenous people within education.[3] The texts presented here shift the focus from trauma-centred to culturally affirming and empowering stories. They share Indigenous voices from across what is now known as North America, including Manitoba, Saskatchewan, Alberta, British Columbia, Northwest Territories, Ontario, and Michigan. Engaging with these positive examples can encourage the cultural healing process and guide educators toward more equitable and sustainable practices in K–12 classrooms and beyond.

In this book, we aim to connect the living curriculum of resurgence that honours Indigenous-centred content and learning processes with classroom and educational practices.

You may have struggled with integrating Indigenous perspectives into your existing curricular plans. We propose that the process be reversed: start here, with the active curriculum of Indigenous voices, stories, and expressions, and listen openly to the curricular potential living within. *Resurgenc* offers support in how to bring these texts into your own learning and your classroom. We treat each piece as a "living text" that acts as a springboard for engaging with Indigenous voices and pedagogies that you can use within professional learning communities and with students of all ages in multiple curricular areas.

---

3   Battiste, "Nourishing the Learning Spirit," 15.

Each text in this book provides a gift that evokes critical reflection on past and current teaching practices and inspires new quests and questions. You can return to these texts again and again, continuing to learn from them over time. Like a footbridge connecting two lands, we hope *Resurgence* provides a path between Indigenous worldviews and your classroom, engaging differences, including tensions, and highlighting the importance of balance and diversity.

Indigenous Pedagogical Approaches

The term *Indigenous* refers to First Nations, Métis, and Inuit communities and peoples collectively. It is important to remember that Indigenous nations are distinct and diverse, and each nation has its own creation stories, languages, ceremonies, and histories. We encourage you to learn about the Indigenous nations whose traditional territories you live and work on. This will help you to avoid taking a pan-Indigenous approach (treating all Indigenous peoples as though they share a single homogeneous culture) when working with Indigenous voices and perspectives.

Having said that, we use the term *Indigenous* to refer to views of teaching and learning that are shared by many Indigenous cultures. In particular, woven throughout this book are pedagogical approaches that support Indigenous ways of teaching and learning: connecting to self, connecting to community, talking back/critical literacy, and inquiry. We've formatted these approaches to fit the trajectory of a unit plan or series of lessons in the Classroom Connections section that follows each text. We suggest beginning by encouraging students to engage with the text, then to personally reflect, reflect with others, engage with the text on a critical level, and finally, delve into an inquiry project to gain mastery or deeper understanding of the concept(s).

We encourage you to engage in these processes, either on your own or in a professional learning community, before bringing this work into your classroom. Once you are comfortable learning through each process, we encourage you to guide students through the same process.

RECONCILIATION

Through *Resurgence*, we are seeking to support educators' ongoing engagement with truth and reconciliation through an increased focus on Indigenous narratives and perspectives. Our work is guided by the Truth and Reconciliation Commission of Canada's Calls to Action, in particular the following:

62. We call upon the federal, provincial, and territorial governments, in consultation and collaboration with Survivors, Aboriginal peoples, and educators, to:

    i. Make age-appropriate curriculum on residential schools, Treaties, and Aboriginal peoples' historical and contemporary contributions to Canada a mandatory education requirement for Kindergarten to Grade Twelve students.

63. We call upon the Council of Ministers of Education, Canada to maintain an annual commitment to Aboriginal education issues, including:

    i. Developing and implementing Kindergarten to Grade Twelve curriculum and learning resources on Aboriginal peoples in Canadian history, and the history and legacy of residential schools.

    ii. Sharing information and best practices on teaching curriculum related to residential schools and Aboriginal history.

    iii. Building student capacity for intercultural understanding, empathy, and mutual respect.

    iv. Identifying teacher-training needs relating to the above.[4]

By learning about the past and committing to a better future, we can work towards reconciliation. We hope *Resurgence* challenges you to reframe your own past and current understandings to see the beauty and intellectual and creative resilience in Indigenous communities.

---

4   Truth and Reconciliation Commission of Canada, *Truth and Reconciliation Commission of Canada: Calls to Action* (2015), publications.gc.ca/collections/collection_2015/trc/IR4-8-2015-eng.pdf.

How This Book Is Organized

This book is organized into four parts:

Part 1: Resistance addresses how Indigenous people have fought against attempts at erasure and assimilation.

Part 2: Resilience highlights the ongoing strength, power, and healing of Indigenous people.

Part 3: Restoring shows efforts to challenge harmful narratives while restoring Indigenous ways of knowing, thinking, and being.

Part 4: Reconnecting encourages and celebrates Indigenous futures.

The part titles emerged naturally from our collaborative reflection and sorting of our contributors' texts based on the topics and content they shared.[1]

Part Overviews: Becoming Story-Ready

Each of the book's four parts opens with an overview that prepares you for the journey across the footbridge that connects Indigenous worldviews and the classroom. The part overviews introduce you to the topics you will engage with; remind you to prepare to listen, read, and view with care; and encourage you to become "story-ready" for the texts that follow.

---

1   Throughout this process, we came across a variety of relevant "R terms" used by writers and scholars, including the renowned Indigenous scholarship of Verna J. Kirkness and Ray Barnhardt, "First Nations and Higher Education: The Four Rs—Respect, Relevance, Reciprocity, Responsibility," in *Knowledge Across Cultures: A Contribution to Dialogue Among Civilizations*, eds. Ruth Hayhoe and Julia Pan (Hong Kong: Comparative Education Research Centre, University of Hong Kong, 2001).

The idea of becoming "story-ready" comes from Indigenous scholar Dr. Jo-ann Archibald Q'um Q'um Xiiem (Stó:lō and St'át'imc).[2] Archibald states that engaging with storywork and learning from stories as a form of pedagogy requires ethical considerations and a sense of their context.[3] While not all of the texts in the book are stories, they are all *storied* in that they provide a window into the contributor's experiences, and the part overviews will help you prepare for the serious work of engaging with them. In each part overview, we focus on four of Archibald's storywork principles for becoming story-ready: respect, responsibility, reverence, and reciprocity.[4] This means "readers must engage with Indigenous stories with respect, develop story relationships in a responsible manner, treat story knowledge with reverence, and strengthen storied impact through reciprocity."[5] As you engage with each text, either on your own or with a community of learners, keep these principles in mind.

In the part overviews, we encourage you to become story-ready in various ways: for example, by drawing attention to topics that may be triggering, offering notes on appropriate language, or sharing which nations contributors are from to help you activate prior knowledge, relationships, or connections. We offer suggestions and prompts to help you prepare your physical space and teaching methods and materials. We encourage you to consider the work you need to do to feel comfortable before approaching these sometimes challenging topics with your students.

---

2   Jo-ann Archibald Q'um Q'um Xiiem, "On Becoming Story-Ready." *Indigenous Storywork*, no date, indigenousstorywork.com/1-for-educators/.

3   Jo-ann Archibald Q'um Q'um Xiiem, "Finding the Bone Needle Through Indigenous Storywork," in *Indigenous Knowledge Systems and Research Methodologies: Local Solutions and Global Opportunities*, eds. Elizabeth Sumida Huaman and Nathan D. Martin (Toronto: Canadian Scholars, 2020).

4   Note that these four principles are part of a set of seven principles, which also includes holism, interrelatedness, and synergy; Jo-ann Archibald Q'um Q'um Xiiem, *Indigenous Storywork: Educating the Heart, Mind, Body, and Spirit* (Vancouver: UBC Press, 2008).

5   Linda Tuhiwai Smith, "Foreword," in *Decolonizing Research: Indigenous Storywork as Methodology*, eds. Jo-ann Archibald, Jenny Lee-Morgan, and Jason De Santolo (London: Zed Books, 2019), 4.

The ideas and advice shared in the part overviews emerged from our collaborative discussions as we learned from each text, and the framework of becoming story-ready helped us connect these examples of resurgence together.

Archibald shares, "As the Elders say, it is more important to listen with 'three ears: two on the sides of our head and the one that is in our heart.'"[6] This reminds us that the texts included in *Resurgence* will evoke strong feelings in our hearts and minds—both positive and challenging. It is important to prepare to listen, so we are mentally, spiritually, physically, and emotionally ready to learn from these texts, and to create an environment where students can do so too. In taking care to prepare, you honour the contributors and the potential of their works to inspire students, ensuring that their texts are brought into educational contexts in ethical ways. Archibald's works remind us that becoming ready to engage with storywork takes time; it is not a checklist to complete but an ongoing journey. We hope these part overviews encourage you to take a purposeful pause after engaging with each text, instead of moving quickly from one to another.

As an educator, you will interpret these texts in unique ways based on who you are, where you come from, what you think and believe, and how you are situated within the power dynamics and problems that are being exposed. It is important to anticipate that your students will also have diverse reactions to the texts and will interpret them in different ways. We encourage you to have an open discussion with your students about what it feels, sounds, and looks like to respect a story. Ask yourself and your students if your own story has ever been retold in a way that did not respect you or your perspective. Consider how that felt and think of how the experience could have been more positive. We encourage you to have an open discussion with your students about how to create a safe space in your classroom for responding to and sharing personal stories. This will help students feel comfortable when participating in the Connecting to Community approach offered in each Classroom Connections section.

---

6   Archibald, *Indigenous Storywork*, 8.

Contributor Biographies

Each contributor's biography is positioned before their text to emphasize that their work and perspectives are integrally connected to place, local knowledge, personal experiences (such as birth and relocation), and where their ancestors are from. Indigenous nations are diverse in their history, language, traditions, and customs, and so are the experiences of Indigenous community members. Read each biography with your class and locate the contributor's ancestral place on a map. They are inviting you into their life and story.

Contributor Narratives and Expressions

Resurgence includes essays, poems, and artwork. Each contributor has used the medium of their choice to communicate their message of resurgence. The many forms of expression used here have the potential to evoke emotions and provoke new possibilities for you to reimagine your professional practices. The table on pages 21–23 lists each contributor, their nation, and their text.

To engage with visual texts with your whole class, we highly encourage you to use a document camera or project them for all to see. Encourage students to record and share their noticings and wonderings as they view these pieces.

Educator Connections

The Educator Connections section presents our thoughts on each text and encourages you to engage in reflection before sharing the text and its topics with your students.[7] The inquiry questions provided here can be used for self-reflection or in discussions with your colleagues in a professional learning community.

PERSONAL CONNECTIONS

After each text, we explore our own personal connections to it in a conversational narrative that describes how the text relates to our lives, our understandings, and our teaching practice. This is an important first step in learning about Indigenous topics, as it forces us to position ourselves in relation to our learning. We ask ourselves the following big questions: How does this relate to me? Who am I in relation to this topic? We hope our responses serve as examples or starting points, and we encourage you to ask yourself these important questions too. Think of our sharing as the beginning of a conversation. Our own reflections are an invitation to you to share a raw response—how do you feel immediately after reading the text? Consider sharing your responses with your students or colleagues.

EDUCATOR INQUIRY AND ACTIONS

Here, we invite you to engage with each text on a personal and professional level. The texts included in the book are quite short, but are loaded with meaning that can encourage deep, rich conversations. We provide guiding questions for inspiration and make suggestions for collaborative inquiry with colleagues—for example, as an action for a professional learning community.

As Rita Bouvier states (p. 44), "calling oneself *teacher* assumes a relationship with the learner(s) and thus carries immense responsibility for

---

7 Although we use the term *educator* here and throughout the book, the Educator Connections section provides opportunities and entry points for any adult learner.

not only the content or knowledge passed on, but also *in practice*." This section guides you in taking on this responsibility, beginning with thinking about your own educational experiences and ongoing learning and then encouraging you to think and take action. It encourages you to ask the following questions of yourself: How am I bringing Indigenous perspectives and voices into my curriculum? What learning do I need to do to support my work with students? Your answers to these questions can be used to guide your actions as you introduce Indigenous voices in your classroom. In schools where we have taught, these questions have also been used to guide action plans for professional learning communities.

Classroom Connections

The Classroom Connections section provides guidance in how to bring these texts into your classroom, offering questions, prompts, and resource suggestions to direct student engagement. This section follows the trajectory of a unit plan, offering support as you encourage your students to move from initially engaging with the text toward a deeper understanding of its subject.

The Footbridge Framework shows how each of the Educator and Classroom Connections sections guides both you and your students toward meaningful engagement with Indigenous voices and texts. The approaches outlined here are steps on the path between your classroom and Indigenous worldviews. The final step in the framework, Beginning a New Journey, asks students to continue to reflect on what they have learned and to carry that knowledge with them as they move forward in engaging with new texts and topics.

Footbridge Framework

EDUCATOR CONNECTIONS

1 Preparing to Set Out

- **Part Overviews:** Think about the part's ideas and themes in relation to "becoming story-ready."

- **Contributor Biographies** and **Contributor Narratives and Expressions:** Focus on the contributor, their relationship to place, and their work.

- **Personal Connections** and **Educator Inquiry and Actions:** Reflect on your personal and professional engagement with Indigenous voices and content.

CLASSROOM CONNECTIONS

2 Leaving Shore

- **Connected Concepts:** Decide on your learning focus. Share the text and its themes with students.

3 Crossing the Bridge

- **Connecting to Self:** Encourage students to engage in personal reflection.

- **Connecting to Community:** Initiate balanced conversations and deepen understanding through learning circles.

- **Talking Back:** Promote critical literacy skills and expose tensions.

- **Inquiry:** Guide students in investigating a question.

4 Reaching the Shore

- **Connections to Indigenous Resources:** Provide suggestions for additional resources or draw on these to support becoming story-ready.

5 Beginning a New Journey

- Encourage students to return to the text with a new lens or read a different text to initiate another journey.

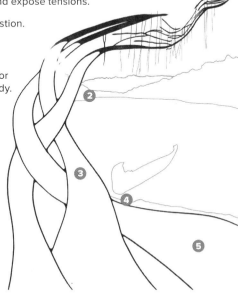

BEGINNING, BRIDGING, AND BEYOND

We understand that your students will engage with the topics explored in the book at varying levels, depending on their own experiences, comfort level, and background knowledge. For this reason, we have indicated that the prompts and questions provided in the Classroom Connections are at a *Beginning*, *Bridging*, or *Beyond* phase. We have opted not to align this content with specific grade levels, which do not necessarily indicate experience with or knowledge of Indigenous topics. The Beginning, Bridging, and Beyond phases are described as follows:

❭ The **Beginning** phase encourages students who are starting out on their journey and have limited experience with or background knowledge of the topic. This phase is indicated by a crescent-moon icon.

❱ The **Bridging** phase is for students with some experience with or background knowledge of the topic. This phase is indicated by a half-moon icon.

● The **Beyond** phase is for students who have extensive experience with or background knowledge of the topic and are ready for more critical and challenging discussions. This phase is indicated by a full-moon icon.

CONNECTED CONCEPTS

This section provides two to four underlying topics that are present in the text. Each text provides many possible interconnections and directions for inquiry, but we have chosen to focus on specific big ideas, or Connected Concepts, for each text. For example, while the broad theme of residential schools is addressed in more than one text, we have highlighted multiple ways of taking up that topic. As you step onto the footbridge with students as they begin their learning journey, share the text and topics you want to focus on with them.

Some of the texts deal with subjects and use language that may not be appropriate for younger students. For these learners, you can focus on exploring the Connected Concepts rather than engaging directly with the text. The broader themes and Connected Concepts are accessible and important to students of all ages. See the table on pages 21–23 for the suggested learner level (which refers to both content and reading level) and Connected Concepts for each text. Be sure to review each text before you introduce it to your students.

The Connected Concepts can also be addressed as stand-alone topics to complement other resources you are using. You can seek out existing provincial or territorial curricula to supplement and expand on specific topics. This will help you ensure that Indigenous voices and expressions are central, rather than an add-on. This approach can help create more meaningful engagement with Indigenous perspectives and knowledges.

CONNECTING TO SELF: PROMPTS FOR PERSONAL REFLECTION

In this section, we offer questions that encourage students to reflect on the text on both personal and academic levels. Here, students begin taking steps across the footbridge toward greater understanding of Indigenous perspectives. For this work to be relevant and to frame action steps, it is important that students consider their own identities. How students demonstrate their learning in this area is up to you; you may invite them to answer questions via written reflection, video reflection, or another mode of assessment. Depending on the topic, you might allow your students to discuss these questions with a partner—a less intimidating option than presenting their views in a whole-class discussion. Note that the questions in the Connecting to Self section are provided at the Beginning, Bridging, and Beyond phases.

One way to encourage self-reflection is to pick a prompt for students to consider when beginning to explore the topic, then to come back to it after some further learning and see if, and how, their thinking has changed over time. Using the frame of *learning* and *unlearning* can help with seeing these changes.[8] Mi'kmaw scholar Marie Battiste calls for us to make a commitment to *unlearning*, which involves gaining awareness of what has unconsciously become the norm in order to "learn new ways of knowing, valuing others, accepting diversity, and making equity and inclusion foundations for all learners."[9]

CONNECTING TO COMMUNITY: PROMPTS FOR LEARNING CIRCLES

Once students have engaged in a process of personal reflection and introspection, the next step on the footbridge is to engage in conversation with community. This opens our eyes to the various ways in which people experience text. By connecting to community, students will learn about the diverse opinions, experiences, and worldviews of those around them.

One way to facilitate these conversations is through a learning circle, also called a talking circle or sharing circle. Talking circles are traditional processes used by many First Nations to ensure everyone has a voice in decision making, whereas learning circles are a reflective classroom activity that encourages respectful communication, active listening, and unity.

While sitting in a circle, everyone (including the adults in the classroom) is equal. In a learning circle, there is a topic of discussion, and speakers are encouraged to speak from the heart on this topic. Only the person holding a designated item, such as a talking stick, may speak, while everyone else listens. Speakers talk until they are finished, being respectful of time. Once the speaker has finished, they pass the stick to the person beside them and that person speaks. Not speaking in a learning circle is acceptable; the person simply says "pass" and passes the item on to the next person. The process is complete when everyone has had a chance to speak. If you want to use learning circles or a similar process with your students, we encourage

---

8   Marie Battiste, "Nourishing the Learning Spirit: Living Our Way to New Thinking," *Education Canada* 50, no. 1 (2010): 14–18, www.edcan.ca/wp-content/uploads/EdCan -2010-v50-n1-Battiste.pdf.

9   Marie Battiste, *Decolonizing Education: Nourishing the Learning Spirit* (Saskatoon: Purich Publishing, 2013), 166.

you to invite a local Elder or Knowledge Keeper into your classroom to share related nation-specific teachings before you do so. Before trying a learning circle in your classroom, you may want to work through the process with colleagues to increase your comfort level and familiarity.

In the Connecting to Community section, we've provided prompts at the Beginning, Bridging, and Beyond phases that can be used in a learning circle. Choose the prompts that are appropriate for you and your students. If you are still getting to know your students, start with the Beginning phase prompts; although these may seem simple, you might be surprised at what surfaces in response! You can keep coming back to these prompts and make them part of your classroom routine. Learning circles are a great outdoor activity too.

CONNECTING ONLINE

To connect with other educators, use our hashtags #FootbridgeResurgence and #FootbridgeResurgenceBook. We encourage you to post reflections from your own learning or share how you take up these ideas in your educational setting!

TALKING BACK

Critical literacy is a key aspect of reading and understanding each text in relation to issues of power, sovereignty, and agency. We emphasize using the strategy of "talking back" when examining each text. This strategy supports Indigenous pedagogical approaches by drawing on critical and engaged pedagogies to critique and examine colonial power structures surrounding the text or colonial impacts shared by the contributors.[10] Each contributor demonstrates their own unique voice and form of talking back in their text.

The practice of talking back connects to the persistent and ongoing actions and courageous creativity of Indigenous communities. One example is Idle No More's ongoing activism to "honour Indigenous sovereignty and to protect the land & water & sky."[11] We encourage you to discuss with your students oppressive Canadian structures, name the key issues that the contributor is in tension with, and be involved in *teaching back* the truths in ways that inspire further action. This process is an important part of the journey across the footbridge toward deeper engagement and understanding.

Throughout *Resurgence* we use two methods of talking back: problem exposing and juxtaposing. These methods support visual literacy skills and thinking critically and from multiple perspectives. Examples of each are offered for every text.

Problem exposing: This section provides an activity to help students expand their perspectives and deepen their understanding of the issues presented in the text. Here, we extend the idea of "problem posing" to focus on exposing the broader structures revealed within each contributor's piece.[12] We encourage you and your students to ask: What are the key issues and tensions that this piece is reacting to? Indigenous content is sometimes introduced in classrooms without naming how it is situated within broader

---

10   For more on "talking back," see Linda Christensen, "Talking Back," in *Beyond Heroes and Holidays: A Practical Guide to K–12 Anti-Racist, Multicultural Education and Staff Development*, eds. Enid Lee, Deborah Menkart, and Margo Okazawa-Rey (Washington, DC: Teaching for Change, 2008); Linda Christensen, *Reading, Writing, and Rising Up: Teaching About Social Justice and the Power of the Written Word* (2nd ed.; Milwaukee, WI: Rethinking Schools, 2017); Peter Kulchyski and Frank Tester, *Kiumajut (Talking Back): Game Management and Inuit Rights, 1900–70* (Vancouver: UBC Press, 2008); Linda Tuhiwai Smith, *Decolonizing Methodologies: Research and Indigenous Peoples* (5th ed.; London: Zed Books, 2002).

11   Idle No More, "Home page," 2020, idlenomore.ca.

12   For more on "problem posing," see Literacy and Numeracy Secretariat, *Critical Literacy* (Special ed. no. 9). Capacity Building Series (Toronto: Ontario Ministry of Education, 2009).

social, historical, and cultural contexts. The "problem exposing" process invites students to name the problem or issue and develop language for talking about the different and increasingly complex ways education systems have impacted, and continue to impact, Indigenous communities. This process helps frame and inspire action-oriented and solution-based extensions and inquiries.

Juxtaposing: Juxtaposition involves pairing two texts (visual, oral, print, or digital media) alongside each other to reveal a new understanding as the texts converse with each other. The activities we have suggested here often begin with images, which can generate rich discussions of complex issues without the pressures of decoding a challenging written text. Juxtaposition can also work to expose a problem in a different way than analyzing just one text; for example: What does the conversation between texts A and B say? What new meanings can be interpreted from the space bridging these two texts?

INQUIRY

The final step in the learning process as students reach the other end of the footbridge is inquiry. In this cumulative step, your students will investigate a topic related to the text by planning, developing, and completing a research project they share with their peers or the wider community.

The inquiry process is compatible with Indigenous perspectives of learning, highlighting the importance of student voice, autonomy, and mastery. In this style of learning, the educator's role moves from content expert to facilitator of a student-directed learning process. Inquiry-based and student-centred approaches are an essential part of learning in the 21st century, helping students gain the ability to apply their knowledge to complex issues.

Students first brainstorm a question they have about the larger themes in the text. To help with this process, we have included examples of inquiry questions at the Beginning, Bridging, and Beyond phases. Students may choose one of these or use them as inspiration for their own inquiry question. Encourage them to choose an open-ended question that fits their experience and level of comfort with the topic. Next, have students find primary and secondary sources that will help them answer their inquiry question. Finally, ask your students to interpret the information they learned and report on their findings. With each prompt, we have included some suggestions for how they might report their findings, but you should encourage your students to make the final decision. The Connecting to Self and Connecting to Community sections offer ideas and reflections that students could use as starting points for their inquiries.

Many of these inquiries are action oriented and focus on advocating for or making changes in the community. As a result, these questions and investigations build on the idea of resurgence as a movement that has momentum, rather than a static concept. Taking action helps keep this momentum going. These suggestions will get students curious and involved.

CONNECTIONS TO INDIGENOUS RESOURCES

Finally, at the end of each chapter, we've included a list of resources (that may include books, films, articles, and online materials) for further investigation and study. As students take their final steps on the footbridge and reach the shore, they may wish to extend their learning by engaging with these suggested works. The texts we've included may address similar topics or may have been created by the contributor or an author or artist from the same nation as the contributor. The suggested books are written by Indigenous authors.

If you think a specific piece in this book is too challenging for your students, but you'd like to teach one of the Connected Concepts, start with one of the age-appropriate resources provided in the Connections to Indigenous Resources section. The age and grade ranges provided for each children's and young adult book are based on the publisher's recommendations.

OVERVIEW OF NARRATIVES AND CULTURAL EXPRESSIONS

The following table provides an overview of each text, specifying the contributor's name and nation, and the title and type of text. Suggested learner level refers to the content and reading level of the text itself; as noted, the Connected Concepts identified for each text can be addressed with students of all ages with various levels of knowledge and experience.

CONTRIBUTOR(S)	CONTRIBUTOR NATION	TITLE OF TEXT	TYPE OF TEXT	SUGGESTED LEARNER LEVEL	CONNECTED CONCEPTS
PART 1: RESISTANCE					
Sara Florence Davidson	Haida	*Beyond Being Silenced*	Essay	Grades 5–12 and beyond	• Roles and responsibilities • Intergenerational learning • Worldview
Rita Bouvier	Métis	*Poetry as a Cultural Expression: if the land could speak*	Essay	Grade 12 and beyond	• Communicating and ways of knowing • Land-based teachings
		"one morning after the rain"	Poem	Grades 5–12 and beyond	• Eurocentrism/ Indigenization
Lucy Hemphill	Kwakw<u>a</u>k<u>a</u>'-wakw	*Ṫse<u>k</u>a Reflection*	Essay	Grades 10–12 and beyond	• Family and connections • Reciprocal relationships
		"Ṫse<u>k</u>a"	Poem	Grades 5–12 and beyond	• Matriarchy
Louise Bernice Halfe	Cree	"Holy Eucharist"	Poem	Grades 8–12 and beyond	• Residential schools
		"miyo kisikaw"	Poem	Grades 8–12 and beyond	• Decolonization • Truth and reconciliation
PART 2: RESILIENCE					
David A. Robertson	Cree	*"Seen in a Good Way": Reading and Writing Through Mental Health Struggles*	Essay	Grades 5–12 and beyond	• Feelings • Representation • Mental health • Resilience
Wanda John-Kehewin	Cree	*Writing as a Therapeutic Medium*	Essay	Grades 10–12 and beyond	• Identity • Voice • Escapism and processing trauma

CONTRIBUTOR(S)	CONTRIBUTOR NATION	TITLE OF TEXT	TYPE OF TEXT	SUGGESTED LEARNER LEVEL	CONNECTED CONCEPTS
KC Adams	Cree/Ojibway	*Birch Bark Technology*	Artist's statement and artwork	Grades K–12 and beyond	• Decoding art • Symbolism in art and Indigenous knowledge
Lisa Boivin	Dene	*Images and Health*	Artist's statement and artwork	Grades 10–12 and beyond	• Body sovereignty • Consent • Systemic racism
PART 3: RESTORING					
Charlene Bearhead and Wilson Bearhead	Nakota	*Stories Are Resurgence*	Essay	Grades 10–12 and beyond	• Sharing stories • Oral storytelling • Telling your story
Sonya Ballantyne	Swampy Cree	*Why Am I Not on* Star Trek?	Essay	Grades 7–12 and beyond	• Representation in literature/media • Role models • Counter-stories
Reanna Merasty	Ininew	*Indigenizing Spaces: Identity in the Built Environment*	Essay	Grades 11 and 12 and beyond	• Traditional and modern Indigenous architecture • Indigenous land acknowledgments • Places and spaces
Elizabeth LaPensée	Anishinaabe/Métis	*Games as Resurgence*	Essay	Grades 11 and 12 and beyond	• Land-based education • Indigenous games • Technology
PART 4: RECONNECTING					
Nicola I. Campbell	Nłeʔkepmx/Syilx/Métis	"alpine mountains"	Poem	Grades 5–12 and beyond	• Memories • Ancestral memory, belonging, and place • Land-based teachings
		"frog whisperers"	Poem	Grades 5–12 and beyond	

CONTRIBUTOR(S)	CONTRIBUTOR NATION	TITLE OF TEXT	TYPE OF TEXT	SUGGESTED LEARNER LEVEL	CONNECTED CONCEPTS
Russell Wallace	Lil'wat7úl	*The Paths of Tradition*	Essay	Grades 8–12 and beyond	• Traditions • Fluidity of culture • Learning through metaphor
Victoria McIntosh	Anishinaabe	*Making a Comeback as an Artist*	Essay	Grades 9–12 and beyond	• Indigenous art/creations • Role of play and joy in learning • Intergenerational stories
		Let the Children Play	Artwork	Grades K–12 and beyond	
Christina Lavalley Ruddy	Algonquin	*We Are Inherently Mathematical*	Essay	Grades 10–12 and beyond	• Beading • Ethnomathematics • Cultural appropriation • Cultural pride

RESISTANCE

PART 1 INITIATES this journey of resurgence by focusing on the theme of resistance. The narratives and poems in this part address oppressive structures and realities and explore how the contributors have transformed profound loss into a powerful reawakening, revival, and continuation of culture.

Many of the narratives and poems in this part address residential schools. Be prepared for the **responsibility** of listening to Louise Bernice Halfe's poetic expressions as a Survivor of Blue Quills Residential School near St. Paul, Alberta.[1] Halfe addresses the intergenerational trauma caused by Indian residential schools; in "Holy Eucharist," she discusses death by suicide, genocide, addiction, and disease through a poetic lens. We have heard the truths uncovered by the Truth and Reconciliation Commission, but poetic forms evoke new understandings and juxtapositions. Ensure you have emotional supports in place prior to reading these powerful pieces. Emotional supports might include debriefing with a colleague, attending therapy, spending time journalling and processing, engaging in a spiritual practice, or doing something that makes you feel well, such as spending time with loved ones or exercising.

Our focus on resistance honours the contributors' complex colonial experiences. The narratives and poems in part 1 call out to you to reflect on your past practices and, as Marie Battiste says, to both "unlearn and

---

1   In each part overview, we focus on four of Indigenous scholar Dr. Jo-ann Archibald Q'um Q'um Xiiem's (Stó:lō and St'át'imc) storywork principles for becoming story-ready: respect, responsibility, reverence, and reciprocity. See Part Overviews: Becoming Story-Ready on page 7 for a description of these principles.

learn—to unlearn the racism and superiority so evident in our society and to learn new ways of knowing, valuing others, accepting diversity, and making equity and inclusion foundations for all learners."[2] Always consider **respectful** language usage as you engage in discussions with colleagues and students; for example, the term *Indigenous peoples* is used to focus on the diversity of Indigenous nations. In this part, you will encounter important terms such as *colonial* and *racialized*. Be prepared to unpack what these mean by researching and learning before introducing them to your students.

In her essay, Rita Bouvier references scholar Emma LaRocque's comment that words are often used to demonize and dehumanize Indigenous experiences.[3] In response to this, ask about terminology when you are unsure, and encourage your students to do so too. Within your classroom, create a space where students can correct each other and where an ongoing dialogue about how language is used is supported. Creating a safe space includes asking students for their input about discussion guidelines and processes for working through challenges in a good way.

Take time to seek out resources for your own reference and to share with your students, like those available through the National Centre for Truth and Reconciliation, including archival material such as photos and the Truth and Reconciliation Commission's Calls to Action and summary report. If you need more background information about a specific nation or culture, seek out appropriate sources. For example, to ensure that you have accurate information and resources regarding the Haida Nation to support Sara Florence Davidson's piece, go directly to the Council of the Haida Nation website <www.haidanation.ca>.

---

2   Marie Battiste, "Nourishing the Learning Spirit: Living Our Way to New Thinking," *Education Canada* 50, no. 1 (2010): 14–18, www.edcan.ca/wp-content/uploads/EdCan -2010-v50-n1-Battiste.pdf.

3   Emma LaRocque, *When the Other Is Me: Native Resistance Discourse 1850–1990* (Winnipeg: University of Manitoba Press, 2010).

Show **reverence** for the many cultural, linguistic, and spiritual traditions of the women writers featured in this part, and the diversity within their powerful words. As an educator, consider how you have helped your students form a learning community that has reverence for multiple perspectives, even those that do not align with your own beliefs. In this part, you will have the opportunity to engage with Haida, Métis, Kwakwaka'wakw, and Cree perspectives. Have you created a space in your classroom that is open to spiritual engagement when learning about sacred practices, such as the cedar bark ceremony described in Lucy Hemphill's essay? Part of this process may be acknowledging your own limitations in understanding.

Here, you will be invited to learn from many teachers—human and more than human, and "so many other living entities" (Bouvier, p. 43). By engaging with these pieces, you are entering into a **reciprocal** relationship to take your learning further, both inside and outside of the classroom. What do you still need to learn about residential schools and their underlying policies, the potlatch ban, the cedar bark ceremony, and so on? How are you bringing diverse Indigenous voices into your curriculum within and beyond the confines of your classroom walls?

Beyond Being Silenced

SARA FLORENCE DAVIDSON (she/her/hers) is a Haida/settler assistant professor in the Faculty of Education at Simon Fraser University. Sara is the co-author of *Potlatch as Pedagogy: Learning Through Ceremony*, which she wrote with her father, Robert Davidson, along with the accompanying Sk'ad'a Stories series of children's picture books focused on Indigenous pedagogies and intergenerational learning.

DURING THE SUMMER of the pandemic,[1] my father finishes a totem pole. He names it *Beyond Being Silenced*. He explains that it is a continuation from the pole *We Were Once Silenced* that he carved several years ago. The first pole was a representation of his understanding of the role of colonialism in the oppression of Indigenous peoples. Specifically, it was an acknowledgment of the pain of the residential school Survivors, including his own father.

With the increased threat of COVID-19, my father's apprentices had returned home to their communities, leaving him safe, but also alone in his studio with no one to help him paint the pole. My father mentions this to me at lunch one day, "putting it out to the universe." My father believes in the power of the universe to help those who are willing to take the first step. In years past, I had painted my brother's panels and my father's canvases; I had never painted a pole. But in our family, we help one another. So, later, I text my father and offer to paint. He quickly accepts my offer.

---

1   This piece was written immediately following the first summer of the pandemic in 2020.

"The vibrancy of the paint brings the pole to life visually, but I can also feel the spirit of the tree continuing to emerge."

On a sunny day in June, I drive to my father's studio to begin painting.

The carved pole lies still in the middle of the plywood floor. I am struck by the thought of the tree's spirit still intact, but it is dormant so I can only catch glimpses of its light as I walk around the pole. Occasionally, I reach out to touch the carved faces. The smell of cedar wafts into the air and lingers in the creases of my palms.

My father provides me with black paint to start. I dip my brush in the container, slide it along the rim to remove excess paint, and then run it along the edges of eyebrows and wings and eventually tail feathers. I think about where my father learned to create these shapes that are older than he is. The knowledge of the Haida form has been passed on to my father from his father, grandfather, and the old Haida masters whose names were never recorded with their art. My father learned from studying the positive and negative spaces in their masterpieces in museums.

As I paint, I can feel the pole begin to awaken. I think back to the stories of the first pole that my father carved and raised in his home community in 1969. It was the first pole raising in almost a century, after the Indian Act was used to assimilate us and force us to stop living our culture. When my parents told me the stories of the Elders gathering to remember the songs and dances and the old way of raising a pole, I could sense the strength that emerged from these gatherings. In my father's words, each Elder held a thread of knowledge, and when they came together it created a thick rope.

I wonder if they too felt a reawakening.

This pole is also the result of the strength that comes from people gathering. My father, my brother, other artists, and apprentices have all carved on this pole. There are even pencil lines that my youngest nephew made as he spent time in the studio watching his father and grandfather carve. Each artist has a skill, and when they came together, they created this pole that reflects all of their strengths. Each artist carries a thread that represents their own learning and connections to the past. This pole has provided an opportunity to bring that knowledge into the present.

My connection to the pole, and the tree it once was, deepens as I spend more time with it in my father's studio. The vibrancy of the paint brings the pole to life visually, but I can also feel the spirit of the tree continuing to emerge. The frogs, grizzly, and eagles carved into the cedar have breathed new life into the tree. The Haida culture that has been carved into the grain has coaxed out the tree's spirit, and now I can feel its energy beginning to radiate from the wood.

During the summer of the pandemic, my brother dies. His death forces me to question my role in keeping the knowledge alive. How can I ensure that what has been passed on to me from generations of ancestors will be passed on to future generations? How can I ensure their spirits will continue to live?

After my brother dies, my father talks to me about the pole. He says he carved the frog at the bottom right away because the frog is his spirit helper. Then he explains that the grizzly and the eagle share a mouth and their tongue speaks over the silence. Together, they draw on the strength of the eagle, who holds the power that we need to regain our voice.

The faces under the tongue remind us of the time that we were silenced. The reminder provides us with inspiration to continue on. At the top of the pole, the three watchmen help us to continue being strong. My father says that we need strength to maintain this new reality, and I cannot help but think of the new reality without my brother.

As I finish painting, I play the old recordings of the Elders singing when they gathered to prepare for the pole raising in 1969. I feel compelled to do this, as if the watchmen are demanding this connection to their past. But then I wonder if perhaps it is the echoes of those Elders from long ago who are calling out to me—reminding me to listen for their guidance.

Either way, I am comforted by the songs.

During that summer, the pole teaches me how to move beyond being silenced. I learn that I must create support for my spirit, for the journey is challenging. I learn that I must find others who hold threads to help me to form a rope. And I learn that I must listen for the voices of my ancestors, because their knowledge ensured their survival and will help me to continue on as well.

From my brother's death, I learn that our spirit continues to live on even when it seems that we are gone.

It continues on through those we taught.

It continues on through those we inspired.

And it continues on through those we loved.

With gratitude to my parents for their contributions to this piece.

We Were Once Silenced,
by Robert Davidson.
(Photo credit: Kenji.)

Beyond Being Silenced,
by Robert Davidson.
(Photo credit: Kenji.)

Educator Connections

Read the editors' thoughts and engage in reflection. Respond to the questions that follow on your own or with your colleague(s).

PERSONAL CONNECTIONS

Christine: I found this personal essay extremely touching and relatable. Sara Florence Davidson expresses that she is awakening to her sense of responsibility in passing down traditional knowledge to future generations; this is something that I think a lot of Indigenous people feel. Our culture and ways of life have been silenced for so long that cultural knowledge isn't common knowledge for a lot of us anymore. Sara Florence Davidson is lucky that her parents and family are able to pass down this knowledge to her. Personally, I too feel an immense responsibility to learn as much about my culture as I can to ensure the transmission of this knowledge into the future. My favourite line in this essay is "I learn that I must find others who hold threads to help me to form a rope," as this is precisely the purpose of this book: to weave together threads of Indigenous expression to strengthen the rope that will guide us over the footbridge into the future.

Katya: The collaboration between Sara Florence Davidson and Robert Davidson made me think about how remarkable it is that Haida knowledges continue on despite multigenerational efforts to silence them. It shows the incredible strength of Haida families and the power of communities working together. What struck me when reading was the way Sara Florence Davidson talked about the tree's spirit within the pole. I think this idea of the tree as a spiritual being with a presence is something that school systems found threatening and dangerous. It makes me think about my past practices when teaching about the West Coast while I was in the Prairies and how disconnected I was from the physical landscapes of mountains, large cedar trees, and the ocean, and the power and presence of the land. This essay teaches me about appropriation and causes me to reflect back on my own practices that did not adequately consider the spiritual dimensions within totem poles.

- How is the theme of resistance portrayed in the text? How have Canadian school systems actively tried to silence Haida knowledges or, more broadly, Indigenous knowledges? How has the Haida Nation, or other Indigenous nations, resisted?

- How do you allow student voice and choice in your classroom? How do you ensure students are not being silenced?

- How does this essay show the revival and continuation of culture amidst both personal and community experiences of loss?

- Reflect on Robert Davidson's belief that "each Elder held a thread of knowledge, and when they came together it created a thick rope." Consider ways you can create a stronger sense of classroom community. As a community, reflect on a specific topic or goal. What do you contribute individually? Share your strengths with the class and listen to the strengths of others. Connect this inquiry to a topic that needs attention in your local or school community. How might all the strengths of the class be used to help brainstorm solutions?

- The Haida Nation is known for its artistic expressions; these are often appropriated. Discuss the difference between *cultural appropriation* and *cultural appreciation* as a school team. When is totem pole art an appropriation of Haida culture? How do you teach about totems and Haida art while maintaining reverence for Haida spirituality and symbolic significance?

Classroom Connections

Introduce to students the narrative and the Connected Concepts you wish to focus on. Use the following questions, prompts, and resource suggestions to guide student learning.

CONNECTED CONCEPTS

- Roles and responsibilities

- Intergenerational learning

- Worldview

CONNECTING TO SELF: PROMPTS FOR PERSONAL REFLECTION

Beginning

- How do family members help each other? What have you learned from your family? What can you teach your family members?

- How does this essay relate to your life?

Bridging

- What information did you learn about Haida culture from this essay?

- What metaphor does the author use in this essay and how does it contribute to your understanding of the significance of the totem pole?

- How does the author talk about community in this essay? What do we learn about the importance of community through this piece?

Beyond

- Have you ever felt silenced? If so, when, and how did you react to this?

- What does the author say about "the role of colonialism in the oppression of Indigenous peoples"?

- What elements of connectedness are shared in this essay?

Beginning

- Share how this essay relates to you and your family.

- Discuss a responsibility you have that you take pride in.

Bridging

- Describe your individual strengths and ways you use these to contribute to a stronger classroom community.

- In this essay, the author discusses her responsibility in passing down knowledge. Share some of the responsibilities that you have in your own life.

- Share how the pandemic has affected you and your family.

Beyond

- Discuss your experience of loss and what personal strengths this revealed.

- Share your thoughts about how this text alludes to larger topics such as colonialism, Indigenous culture, the transmission of knowledge, and resistance.

- Describe how knowledge is passed on in your family, considering if and how knowledge has been lost over time.

TALKING BACK

Sara Florence Davidson's personal essay is talking back to the effects of attempted cultural genocide and how families have taken responsibility for supporting the revival of their culture. This text reveals key tensions surfacing from the Indian Act, residential schools, and colonial policies.

- **Problem exposing:** This essay highlights how art is used to represent understandings of "generational pain" caused by colonial policies. The act of cross-generational collaborations (such as between Sara Florence Davidson and her father, Robert Davidson) actively works against these oppressive systems.

Use the arts to demonstrate your understanding of how the Canadian government has silenced Haida people (or Indigenous peoples in your local context) and how communities have moved "beyond being silenced." This could take the form of visual art, slam poetry, a song, or another medium of your choice.

- **Juxtaposing:** Look at the images of the totem poles *We Were Once Silenced* and *Beyond Being Silenced*. Consider questions such as the following: What do you see, notice, and wonder about how these are similar or different? How have positive and negative spaces been reflected? What do these totem poles teach about oppressive realities?

INQUIRY

Beginning

- What is a totem pole and why do you believe it is significant to Haida people? Look at images of totem poles (for example, from Robert Davidson's website <www.robertdavidson.ca>) while thinking about this art form and the imagery described in the essay. Listen to Haida artists and Knowledge Keepers describe the significance of totem poles in their own voices.

- Explore cultural shapes and designs. How have Haida artists used positive and negative space in their works? How is this practised by artists in other places? Consider the significance of Robert Davidson creating "shapes that are older than he is." What shapes have been passed down for generations within the cultures you identify with?

Bridging

- What is the history and ongoing legacy of the Haida people? Create a visual timeline to show your learning about how Haida culture has been impacted by colonization and how it has thrived.

- This piece exposes a difference in worldviews: trees as commodities versus trees as spiritual beings. View images of logging from British Columbia to guide discussions about how some worldviews and practices affect the natural environment. How do these compare to Haida cultural practices and teachings?

Beyond

- How was knowledge passed down through generations in Haida culture? Think about this guiding question as you look at the Connections to Indigenous Resources or other Haida resources. What are some of the connections you notice that move across the resources and across generations?

- How has COVID-19 affected Indigenous communities across Canada during the first years of the pandemic? Look at news stories that represent both challenges and positive or surprising outcomes.

CONNECTIONS TO INDIGENOUS RESOURCES

Books

Sk̲'ad'a Stories series, by Sara Florence Davidson and Robert Davidson (HighWater Press, 2021–2022; ages 6–8/grades 1–3).
The stories in this series connect to the theme of intergenerational learning, focusing on learning through observation and the role of Elders in sharing knowledge and mentorship.

Potlatch as Pedagogy: Learning Through Ceremony, by Sara Florence Davidson and Robert Davidson (Portage & Main Press, 2018).
This Haida resource, by the contributor and her father, details the potlatch ban and documents the Davidsons' efforts to reclaim their ceremonies, describing how these practices were revived.

Out of Concealment: Female Supernatural Beings of Haida Gwaii, by Terri-Lynn Williams-Davidson (Heritage House, 2017).
This book presents the origin stories of the Haida Nation through vibrant depictions of its female supernatural beings. This book features over 30 full-colour photo collages by Haida artist, performer, and activist Williams-Davidson.

Film

Haida Modern, directed by Charles Wilkinson (Knowledge Network, 2019). <www.knowledge.ca/program/haida-modern>.

This documentary, ideal for high school students, explores Robert Davidson's art and activism. The totem pole that Davidson is carving in this documentary is *Beyond Being Silenced*.

Online

"Raising the Issues with the 'Family Totem Pole'" and "Raven Bringing Light to the World," by Sara Florence Davidson. <saraflorence.ca/blog>.

In these two blog posts, Sara Florence Davidson addresses the issue of cultural appropriation. In the first, she looks at important considerations for educators bringing Indigenous culture into their classrooms; in the second, she writes about Prime Minister Justin Trudeau's tattoo, which is an altered design of an original work created by her and her father.

Poetry as a Cultural Expression: if the land could speak[1] and "one morning after the rain"

RITA BOUVIER, a Métis educator, formally served 37 years in public education as a classroom teacher and in various leadership capacities locally, nationally, and internationally. She was awarded an Eagle Feather from her Awasis peers in 2006, the Saskatchewan Teachers' Federation Arbos Award in 2007, and the Indspire Award for Education in 2014. Rita's poetry collection *nakamowin'sa for the seasons* (Thistledown Press, 2015) was the 2016 Saskatchewan Book Awards' winner of the Rasmussen, Rasmussen, and Charowsky Aboriginal Peoples' Writing Award.

———

ORDS ARE OFTEN used to demonize and dehumanize our experience as Indigenous people in colonial and racialized texts.[2] We also know from our storytelling traditions that *words* are transformative and can be used to weave a human story of purpose and survival—one that acknowledges culturally diverse ways of knowing, being,

---

1 This essay is borrowed in part and in whole segments from *if the land could speak* (unpublished), prepared for a panel address on "Body, Memory, Language" at the Indigenous Intervention into the "Indigenous Narrative" Conference held at the Institute of Indigenous American Arts, Santa Fe, New Mexico, in 2016.

2 Emma LaRocque, *When the Other Is Me: Native Resistance Discourse 1850–1990* (Winnipeg: University of Manitoba Press, 2010).

"When the consciousness embedded in Indigenous languages is shared, spoken, and heard, the land speaks to us."

and seeing in the world to address the frailties of human existence in a living, dynamic universe. Knowing this, how does one give expression to one's existence and make whole again one's aliveness in the world?

Poetry, as an artistic imaginative expression of one's experience in the world, is one strategy. However, words are only one aspect of language; languages also encompass culturally significant performative measures that can be used to give perspective and meaning on the page and in oral recitation.[3]

I grew up on an island, known to the local people as Île Bouleau in my home community of sâkitawak, or Île-à-la-Crosse in Saskatchewan. We spoke Michif—a language that integrates different languages. Linguistically, the Michif of my home community is Cree based (y-dialect borrowed from the Cree inhabiting the region) with French nouns *thrown in for good measure*,[4] often combining the grammatical rules of both languages.[5] The language of instruction at school was English before I had learned to speak, read, and write in the language. The languages I speak are framed by distinct worldviews, each providing me with insight into my experience in a world I share with so many other living entities—human and otherwise.

When the consciousness embedded in Indigenous languages is shared, spoken, and heard, the land speaks to us. Our languages carry the memories and ethos of place—the mnemonic-sonic sounds of our relatives, and the sacred laws governing life and our relationships. Our active, verb-based languages also remind us everything is alive and changing. When we listen deeply, *our mother's movement and voice* touches us, shaping our consciousness and imagination. Our languages are an indispensable part of being from this place we know as Turtle Island, and the etymology—the knowledge gained through study of our languages—is a gift that belongs to all of us.

---

3 Dell Hymes, *"In Vain I Tried to Tell You": Essays in Native American Ethnopoetics* (Lincoln & London: University of Nebraska Press, 2004).

4 Rita Bouvier, *Blueberry Clouds* (Saskatoon: Thistledown Press, 1999).

5 Peter Bakker, *A Language of Our Own: The Genesis of Michif, the Mixed Cree-French Language of the Canadian Métis* (New York: Oxford University Press, 1997).

I am okiskinahamâkêw—a teacher. Exploring the philosophical signif-icance of this statement would be a separate undertaking. It is enough to write that I have learned—listening to and reading works of Paulo Freire—that calling oneself *teacher* assumes a relationship with the learner(s) and thus carries immense responsibility for not only the content or knowl-edge passed on, but also *in practice*. I have also learned the etymology of okiskinahamâkêw—one who shows the way (loosely translated as "teacher" in English)—from my late stepfather, Louis Opikokew. The root word of this polysynthetic word, he noted in a conversation with me, is "one who looks to the future," thus meaning "one who shows the way with future genera-tions in mind." In this time of reconciliation and resurgence, teachers have incredible opportunity to create a powerful learning environment for all their students with the choices they make in bringing the voices of Indige-nous writers to the fore as part of the curriculum and their practice.

Writing poetry is both a means and an end. It provides the means to transcend and navigate the oppressive conditions that have rendered Indig-enous peoples' intellectual traditions as lacking depth and/or as obsolete. It provides an end to humanize my experience (lived and imagined) and to connect with others. I do so by remembering (ikiskisiyan mana) knowl-edge passed down to me, by dreaming (ipôwâtaman), by gathering strength (isôkitaman mina) and resisting and reconciling what has happened and is happening to our families and communities and to the natural environment, and most importantly by rejoicing (imiyowâtaman) in the one life given to me. In a creative poetic reprise, I often find myself returning to place and to the sounding—the music of our mother's movement and voice. We are all related—kahkiyaw iwâhkôhtoyak.

As an educator and a writer, I have opportunities to weave together my cultural story as a Métis woman living in Canada and my Indigenist/feminist concerns and acts of resistance, albeit with difficulty on occasion. Retired, I continue to support the work of communities and organizations promoting lifelong learning and well-being for our communities. Chal-lenging the material and imaginative failures of colonial policies resulting in genocide—extermination through residential schools, displacement, depopulation through disease, neglect, and the continuing marginalization of our knowledge systems and languages through an imposed Eurocentric education is difficult work, as is undoing its effects in our communities.[6]

For example, reconciling the complicity of Catholic priests in our struggles as Métis people to hold on to a land base in the northwest region of Canada prior to the creation of Manitoba, Saskatchewan, and Alberta as provinces is challenging. However, it was important to do so because of the respect and love I had for my grandmother. Her faith in the goodness of humanity was unwavering, especially for those who dedicated their lives to kisîman'tô—the kind, loving creator of all. In "a letter to a friend," I imagined how a priest complicit in the land grab reconciles his own humanity.[7] The poem is dedicated to my grandmother.

What sustains me in my work and my writing is the foundation of love fostered in my early education, naming the world guided by people who loved me, and a language embedded with an ethos of being in relationship with all the people and life around me. Words naming my relationships are preceded with ni—my, nimama—my mother. This is a space where squirrels are relatives. This is a time when, if it rained, my grandparents would say: Îmatôt—she/he/they are crying. tâpwê—I am telling you the truth! And such truths were underscored as I have done.

School, of course, challenged every aspect of this learning. Eventually, I learned to navigate and live in this complex and challenging environment, but not without loss and a pervading sense of longing. Through "education"—credentialed, self-directed—but most'v through dialogue with others of like mind and heart, I learned how entren__'d and entangled Eurocentric and hierarchical thinking was and is in our lives: in law, in economics, in science, in religion, and in so-called history reinforced through education systems.

---

6   Gregory Cajete, *Indigenous Community: Rekindling the Teachings of the Seventh Fire* (St. Paul, MN: Living Justice Press, 2015).

7   Rita Bouvier, *papîyâhtak* (Saskatoon: Thistledown Press, 2004).

On more than one occasion, the relationship fostered with *the great mystery* in my mother tongue has been my salvation. It helps to think through situations in my first language, even though my education/learning in that language ended abruptly when I was 13 years of age, leaving a pervading sense of loss and longing. Indigenous narratives—the thinking offered by Indigenous scholars and writers—are important to the well-being of our communities, and perhaps to the well-being of our planet. Indigenous peoples' intellectual and imaginative engagement has made a significant dent in the dominant Eurocentric consciousness permeating the globe—thinking based on a hierarchy of being, on racial and gender-bound exclusions as rational to displace people from place, their lands, their languages, and their identities, and then reinforced through history,[8] systems, and institutions.

Sadly, the nexus of this predominant Western philosophical tradition has been science, sometimes with religion not far behind.[9] This is not to suggest that the knowledge and wisdom that come from the tradition of the sciences and spiritual dimensions of religions have nothing to offer us. My own community and nation, the Métis, were not averse to *borrowing* the best of all the intellectual traditions presenting themselves through kinship and love of the land that gave them life.[10] I note *sadly* because science—read as a study of "the natural world"—*is* the foundation of the core values and teachings of Indigenous peoples worldwide, and it *is* at the core of our spirituality.

For these reasons, it is important to give voice to our ancestors (literally and figuratively), to resist thinking that denigrates our relationships with others and to all life, and to create anew our visions and understandings of a living, dynamic, and interrelated universe as we imagine a better future for all our children. nitanis kimâmitonihcikan âpacitâh echoes in my ear; it

---

8 Linda Tuhiwai Smith, *Decolonizing Methodologies: Research and Indigenous Peoples* (London: Zed Books, 1999).

9 Vine Deloria, *Evolution, Creationism and Other Modern Myths* (Golden, CO: Fulcrum Publishing, 2002).

10 Signa A. K. Daum Shanks, "Searching for Sakitawak: Place and People in Northern Saskatchewan's Île-à-la-Crosse" (PhD thesis, University of Western Ontario, 2015), ir.lib .uwo.ca/etd/3328.

is my grandfather, the late Joseph Bouvier, speaking to me in relationship, reminding me to use the power of my mind and imagination.

Poetry as a cultural expression of a lived life in a messed-up world provides insights on how to reconcile transgressions of our sacred lives by creating anew and by remembering to live in this place and time with grace, love, joy, and belongingness.

one morning after the rain[11]

her breath a whisper she awakens her brood
wild creatures in first light, her offering
a song of songs   only birds can sing.
hillside, a light mist clings, covering her face.

the early light catches each strand   of grass
swaying in the breeze   imitating the flow of life.
the grass dance is sure to begin, but not
until the night hawk on his perch   rests.

in glory blood red, sky blue, grass yellow
dancers will whirl and whirl and whirl a circle
in honour of her beauty.   humbled.
a winged mid-flight embrace of birds is a reminder

they know this place better than anyone. she cries
in relief when rains come, knowing all is well.

---

11 This poem was originally published in *nakamowin'sa for the seasons*, by Rita Bouvier
(Thistledown Press, 2015, p. 29). In the book, the following note accompanies the poem:
"On the side of a sandstone cliff in south-central Saskatchewan, Canada are petroglyphs
of several symbols—human and animal. After a rain, a time when the petroglyphs appear
to show up more clearly, a petroglyph of a stylized human face appears to be crying. I am
curious. Why?"

Educator Connections

Read the editors' thoughts and engage in reflection. Respond to the questions that follow on your own or with your colleague(s).

PERSONAL CONNECTIONS

Christine: Rita Bouvier's essay is an incredibly powerful reminder of the importance of questioning the assumptions we take for granted as "truth" in education that are based on colonial worldview. For example, I am immediately reminded of how in Anishinaabemowin, words are categorized as animate (living) or inanimate (non-living). What's interesting to me—as a late language learner—is that we have words like *rock* that are categorized as animate. The teaching I've learned is that this is because when we enter our sweat lodges, we use grandfather rocks to communicate with the spirits. This leads me to understand how the essence of our language embeds a reverence for the land and all its inhabitants. As an English teacher, I am responsible for naming and questioning the use of language to further colonize, racialize, and dichotomize thought.

Katya: Rita Bouvier shows the complexities of reconciliation by highlighting all the many internal and external structures of coloniality that have the power to divide, displace, and distance. It makes me think about how much I still have to learn as a teacher. I feel an increasing responsibility to think about how I live out the role of teacher in a meaningful way. How do I not only acknowledge the systems of oppression that I am part of, but also recentre Indigenous narratives, words, and languages in my practices to unlock intellectual and imaginative possibilities and mysteries that are key to the "well-being of our planet"? The idea of the land speaking and languages speaking to the relationship of land makes me recognize how land is a teacher, and through the reclamation of languages, communities can also renew connections with land. I think about language loss within my own family and what worldviews have been instilled within me through language. I want to continue to live and learn in ways that honour more holistic connections.

- What does Rita Bouvier say about education and the role of being a teacher?

- How are worldviews reflected in how you teach languages and multi-literacies?

- Think about the truths spoken by the land. What does the land teach us about ourselves, each other, and community? Zoom into Rita Bouvier's poem "one morning after the rain" as a starting point.

- How can words be used to hurt, help, or heal? In your classroom, how do you nurture and teach about respectful language and its connection to students' cultural, linguistic, and gender identities?

- Reflect on your role as an educator. Do you challenge colonial policies or Eurocentric educational practices through this role? If so, how?

- How can poetry be used to develop a sense of belonging to a particular place (or of "returning to place")? Resist the urge to answer this question quickly and instead take time to ruminate and draft your response in poetic form.

- Find an example of colonial or divisive language currently used in your local, personal, and school community or everyday environments. How can you expose this and reimagine alternatives?

Classroom Connections

Introduce to students the narrative and poem and the Connected Concepts you wish to focus on. Use the following questions, prompts, and resource suggestions to guide student learning.

- Communicating and ways of knowing

- Land-based teachings

- Eurocentrism/Indigenization

CONNECTING TO SELF: PROMPTS FOR PERSONAL REFLECTION

⟩ Beginning

- What is "one morning after the rain" describing and what do you think about it?

- Create a drawing as you listen to your teacher read "one morning after the rain" aloud. Can you describe what your drawing represents?

- What is your favourite way to express yourself and communicate with others?

⟩ Bridging

- What information did you learn about Métis culture from Rita Bouvier's essay? What do you want to learn more about?

- How would you describe the mood of "one morning after the rain"?

⬤ Beyond

- What does Rita Bouvier say about her Métis language in this essay? What questions do you have for her?

- What are some of the poetic devices Rita Bouvier uses in "one morning after the rain"?

- What are some examples of varying worldviews?

> **Beginning**

- Share words that you love and words that bother you and why this matters to you.

- Discuss what it means to live with "grace, love, joy, and belongingness," and describe what you imagine when you think of this.

> **Bridging**

- Discuss your experiences learning a language. Share a word in a language other than English and teach about its meaning and how it is used.

- Share a story about a time you expressed yourself in a way that resisted something—for example, naming a racist comment, rallying on an issue, or responding to an injustice.

> **Beyond**

- Discuss the idea of worldviews, ways they are embedded in languages, and how they affect people and societies.

- In her essay, Rita Bouvier asks, "how does one give expression to one's existence and make whole again one's aliveness in the world?" Describe how you prefer to express yourself and why.

TALKING BACK

Rita Bouvier is talking back to how colonial language seeps into consciousness and affects how one sees the world and one's place and connections within it.

- **Problem exposing:** Rita Bouvier's essay exposes the "messed-up" colonial, racialized, constructed world and describes the entanglement of Eurocentric thinking in our lives. Her poetry is a way of talking back to views of knowledge as static and fixed versus dynamic and living; it "provides the means to transcend and navigate the oppressive conditions that have rendered Indigenous peoples' intellectual traditions as lacking depth and/or as obsolete." Take a walk outside (in either a rural or urban environment). Listen to what the land might be saying as you walk.

Sketch or jot notes of sensory words, feelings, and wonderings. Use your choice of poetic form to share what you heard.

- **Juxtaposing:** Find an image that demonstrates an ongoing "land grab" (for example, fracking, mining, urban sprawl, Métis scrip). Position this alongside "one morning after the rain." What do you notice? What do you wonder? Consider land as a text: What do the representations of land in the image and the poem say to each other?

INQUIRY

> **Beginning**

- Consider an inquiry into pronouns and using pronouns to identify oneself. Explore your own pronoun possibilities and how you choose to identify. How are languages gendered or non-gendered?

- What do you want to learn about Métis culture and the Michif language? Consider why the Canadian government wanted Indigenous people to speak only English and French.

- Read the note that accompanies "one morning after the rain" and look into the cultural significance of pictographs or petroglyphs in an Indigenous place or location to initiate an inquiry. It would be ideal to have the support of an Indigenous Elder or Knowledge Keeper to guide you. Resources such as *Manitowapow: Aboriginal Writings From the Land of Water* can also help with understanding the significance of petroglyphs and storied landscapes.[12]

---

12 Niigaanwewidam James Sinclair and Warren Cariou, eds., *Manitowapow: Aboriginal Writings From the Land of Water* (Winnipeg: Portage & Main Press, 2012).

- What do you notice from being in and with nature? Take a walk and listen, draw, write, and talk about what you see, hear, and feel. Then zoom in to a topic. Which words stand out? Convey your feelings and movements with not only the words, but also the space and layout of the printed text.

- Consider an inquiry into several terms across multiple languages to help understand how worldviews are embedded within words.

- Write dual-language poems using digital translation tools or by asking people in your community to translate key words into an Indigenous language used in your territory. Share your work and reflect on what new meanings you discovered along the way.

● **Beyond**

- What do the terms *colonial* and *racialized* mean to you? Use visuals or poetry to represent your inquiry and understandings.

- What has been the impact of European arrival on Indigenous languages? How are languages changing? How are languages being reclaimed/revitalized? Pick a local Indigenous language and research its history. Seek out someone who speaks or is learning the language and ask them to share their perspective.

- Rita Bouvier shares that Western philosophical traditions focus on science, but Indigenous knowledges were portrayed as disconnected from the sciences. How is science at the core of Indigenous knowledges and spirituality?

CONNECTIONS TO INDIGENOUS RESOURCES

Books

Trudy's Healing Stone, by Trudy Spiller (Medicine Wheel Education, 2019; ages 4–6/grades K–1).

This book tells the story of a girl who learns to deal with difficult emotions with the help of Mother Earth.

Siha Tooskin Knows the Nature of Life, by Charlene Bearhead and Wilson Bearhead (HighWater Press, 2020; ages 9–11/grades 3–5).
This book shows how Ena Makoochay (Mother Earth) is a teacher, as the main character, an 11-year-old Nakota boy, learns about strength, generosity, kindness, and humility.

A Girl Called Echo series, by Katherena Vermette (HighWater Press, 2018–2021; ages 12–14/grades 7–8).
This graphic novel series follows a 13-year-old Métis girl as she travels back in time to experience important historical events first-hand.

Indigenous Writes: A Guide to First Nations, Métis, and Inuit Issues in Canada, by Chelsea Vowel (HighWater Press, 2016).
In this book of essays exploring Indigenous experience from contact to the present, Vowel takes a deeper look at topics such as Métis identity and the origins of Michif.

Manitowapow: Aboriginal Writings From the Land of Water, edited by Niigaan-wewidam James Sinclair and Warren Cariou (Portage & Main Press, 2012).
This anthology of Indigenous writings from Manitoba includes descriptions of the significance of petroglyphs.

"Our matriarchs kept our
ceremonies and stories alive."

T́seḵa Reflection and "T́seḵa"

LUCY HEMPHILL is a Kwakwaḵa'wakw mother from the Gwa'sala-'Nakwaxda'xw Nation. She graduated from the University of British Columbia with a Bachelor of Arts in First Nations and Indigenous Studies in 2019. Lucy strives to reconnect to ancestral relational ways of being and is currently working to develop language revitalization and healing programs in her community. Lucy is the author of the Overhead Series, which includes three poetry titles: *Clouds*, *Stars*, and *Trees*.

FOR THE KWAKWAḴA'WAKW, the ṗasa, often referred to as "potlatch," is the realm where our social, political, legal, and ceremonial duties are carried out. Most importantly, it's where we honour, maintain, and strengthen our reciprocal relationships to one another, to the land and sea, and to the ones who have come before us. From 1884 to 1951, the Canadian government made it illegal to carry out our ceremonies, including the ṗasa. This was an attempt to destroy the Kwakwaḵa'wakw way of life, so that we could be assimilated and moved onto small reserves and our territories could be accessed by fishing, logging, and mining companies for capitalistic gain. My own people—the Gwa'sala-'Nakwaxda'xw—now live on a small reserve, Tsulquate, in the territories of the Kwagu'ł on the northern tip of Vancouver Island. The Canadian government forcibly relocated us from our territories on Mainland British Columbia in 1964. Our ceremonies look a lot different than they did prior to the potlatch ban and the relocation. Yet they still exist.

Prior to the COVID-19 pandemic, our people gathered many times during the year to attend these ceremonies. The t́seḵa, or cedar bark ceremony, is a sacred ceremony carried out in the ṗasa. This ceremony begins with four chiefs holding a circle of red cedar bark around a matriarch from the potlatching family. After the chiefs and the matriarch circle the floor four times, one of the chiefs tries to sever the cedar bark ring. He strikes three times but does not sever the cedar bark until the fourth strike. At that time, the young women of the family distribute red cedar bark strips to wear for the duration of the t̓se<u>k</u>a ceremony to keep guests safe while they witness the ceremony.

In my family, as with many among the Kwakw<u>a</u>ka'wakw, our matriarchs kept our ceremonies and stories alive. They nurtured the reciprocal relationships that are integral to who we are. This poem, "T̓se<u>k</u>a," is an acknowledgment of the sacred relationships they kept alive for us all. Like the cedar, the tree of life, they were and are the pillars of our families and society. Like the cedar tree, they have given and continue to give generously. Moreover, this piece is an acknowledgment of our responsibility as Kwakw<u>a</u>ka'wakw to carry on their important work.

T̓se<u>k</u>a

a forest of stories woven into these bones
warp and weft
deepest red
the colour of blood at moon time
strong but soft
love not weakness
the blade will only sever what we choose
life flows through us
death flows too
our roots run deep and out of harm's reach
kept safe from lies
wrapped in cedar bark
the strength of women who came before us
like tree sap, runs through these veins

Educator Connections

Read the editors' thoughts and engage in reflection. Respond to the questions that follow on your own or with your colleague(s).

PERSONAL CONNECTIONS

Christine: For me, this piece is a reminder of the importance of women in our communities. Hemphill explains how the matriarchs in her family kept the ceremonies and stories alive. I am reminded of the matriarchs in my family—my mom and aunties—who kept our family united and strong. This piece forces me to ask myself: How will I carry on this responsibility one day?

Katya: I am learning about the importance of cedar within ceremony. I am learning that my education regarding the potlatch on the West Coast was hollow. I was not taught about the many nations and traditions of the West Coast. I am amazed at the strength of women and how the Kwakwa̱ka'wakw ceremonies have adapted and survived despite relocation, a potlatch ban, and colonial attempts of cultural genocide.

EDUCATOR INQUIRY AND ACTIONS

- What are you learning from Lucy Hemphill? What does reading about the cedar bark ceremony teach you?

- What do "reciprocal relationships" mean in your personal and professional life?

- How might you foster more awareness of and engagement in reciprocity with students? With families and communities?

- Reflect on your rituals, routines, or traditions as an educator, and as a family and community member. How are these similar to or different than the ones in this piece?

- How might you create a learning environment that respects land as a relative? What do you need to learn more about to engage with this topic with students?

- As a school team, think about how you might bring into the school cultural practices (with the support of community members and Knowledge Holders) as a way of restoring those that were purposefully banned. Make a plan and invite parents and community members to share their ideas.

Classroom Connections

Introduce to students the narrative and poem and the Connected Concepts you wish to focus on. Use the following questions, prompts, and resource suggestions to guide student learning.

CONNECTED CONCEPTS

- Family and connections

- Reciprocal relationships

- Matriarchy

CONNECTING TO SELF: PROMPTS FOR PERSONAL REFLECTION

⟩ **Beginning**

- What is a family? Who is in your family? What are the roles of each member of your family?

- How can we treat Mother Earth and the land as a relative?

- Can you think of examples of relationships where both members benefit?

> **Bridging**

- What is a reciprocal relationship? What are some examples of reciprocal relationships you have with the land, animals, and other people?

- What do land and trees give to you and how do you give back?

● **Beyond**

- What does the ṫseḵa/cedar bark ceremony teach you or make you wonder?

- How is the strength of the community (particularly women) revealed in *Ṫseka Reflection*?

- What symbols or imagery of resistance, resurgence, or reciprocity can you find in the poem?

CONNECTING TO COMMUNITY: PROMPTS FOR LEARNING CIRCLES

> **Beginning**

- Share a story or lesson you learned from the land and how you learned this lesson or teaching.

- Share how you are connected to the land.

> **Bridging**

- Describe a matriarch or woman leader in your life who inspires you.

- Share a metaphor or simile that describes your understanding of the role of a person who inspires you. For example, when Lucy Hemphill describes the matriarchs in her family, she says, "Like the cedar, the tree of life, they were and are the pillars of our families and society."

● **Beyond**

- Discuss what the term *reciprocity* means to you in your life.

- Share a cultural practice or tradition you partake in and describe what values it instills.

Lucy Hemphill's essay and poem address the adaptation and continuation of Kwakwa̱ka'wakw ceremonies despite relocation and share the significant role of women in talking back to this by keeping sacred ceremonies and knowledges alive.

- **Problem exposing:** This essay and poem describe colonial attempts to displace the Kwakwa̱ka'wakw and to eradicate cultural practices, ceremonies, and ways of life. Look into other stories of the Kwakwa̱ka'wakw and how their experiences were similar to and different from other nations within the provincial territory of British Columbia.

- **Juxtaposing:** Compare and contrast the potlatch process with the procedure used in a government process (for example, the legislative process). Consider: How is wealth, or power, viewed and distributed? How are relationships forged and maintained? How are women involved?

In "T̓seka," Lucy Hemphill writes, "the blade will only sever what we choose." How is the purposeful and careful severing of the cedar bark ring juxtaposed with the thoughtless severing of forests in British Columbia?

INQUIRY

) Beginning

- How does the land support us? How do we support the land and nurture this reciprocal relationship? Create a brochure or an online video to showcase how we can be better stewards of the land.

- Who are the Kwakwa̱ka'wakw and where are they from? Use digital resources and online mapping to look at traditional territories and small reserve territories where communities were relocated.

) Bridging

- How did matriarchs keep ceremonies and stories alive for the Kwakwa̱ka'wakw? Look into other matriarchal cultures and the role of women across various societies.

- What was happening in Canada from 1884 to 1951? How does this compare and contrast with what was happening in Tsulquate on Vancouver Island?

- **Beyond**
  - Look at other historical and contemporary examples of relocation from coast to coast. Look at relocations within your own specific place. Who benefitted? How was land used?

  - Research resistance movements aimed at protecting the land from resource development.

  - Engage in an inquiry project about Traditional Ecological Knowledge (TEK).[1]

CONNECTIONS TO INDIGENOUS RESOURCES

Books

Stand Like a Cedar, by Nicola I. Campbell (HighWater Press, 2021; ages 3-5/grades K-2).
This story shares the sights, sounds, and teachings from animals, the land, and waters in Nłeʔkepmxcín or Halq'eméylem languages, complementing the topic of reciprocal relationships and adding to students' understanding of the diversity of languages and perspectives on the West Coast of Canada.

Mothers of Xsan series, by Hetxw'ms Gyetxw Brett D. Huson (HighWater Press, 2017-; ages 9-11/grades 4-6).
This series centres on animal mothers (including an eagle, frog, and sockeye salmon), depicting their life cycles and the interconnections and reciprocal relationships between ecosystems.

---

1 See Robin Wall Kimmerer, "Weaving Traditional Ecological Knowledge into Biological Education: A Call to Action." *BioScience* 52, no. 5 (May 2002): 432–438, doi .org/10.1641/0006-3568(2002)052[0432:WTEKIB]2.0.CO;2.

"Tilted Ground," by Sonny Assu, from *This Place: 150 Years Retold* (HighWater Press, 2019; ages 15–18/grades 9–12).
Told in graphic novel form, this story of the author's great-great-grandfather shows how he maintained Kwakwa̲ka'wakw practices when they were banned by the Canadian government.

Discovery Passages, by Garry Thomas Morse (Talonbooks, 2011).
This collection of poems demonstrates a resurgence of Kwakwa̲ka'wakw culture, tracing routes and roots of colonization through the islands of the West Coast. "500 Lines," the book's final poem, is a versatile text that engages with the ideas of schooling, colonization, and language loss.

Online
"The Potlatch Ban," Simon Fraser University: Bill Reid Institute.
<www.sfu.ca/brc/online_exhibits/masks-2-0/the-potlatch-ban.html>.
This resource provides historical information, and includes photo galleries of masks; descriptions of cultural practices such as tattoos, spruce root weaving, and carving of red cedar dance screens; and short videos.

"Living Tradition: The Kwakwa̲ka'wakw Potlatch on the Northwest Coast," U'Mista Cultural Society (2021). <umistapotlatch.ca/intro-eng.php>.
This website provides a variety of multimodal resources about the potlatch, including a virtual tour and videos.

"Holy Eucharist"
and "miyo kisikaw"

LOUISE BERNICE HALFE, also known by her Cree name, Sky Dancer, is Canada's ninth parliamentary poet laureate. She was raised on Saddle Lake First Nation and attended Blue Quills Residential School. Louise served as the first Indigenous poet laureate of Saskatchewan, and earned her Doctorate of Letters from Wilfrid Laurier University, the University of Saskatchewan, and Mount Royal University. Louise's most recent titles include *awâsis—kinky and dishevelled* and a new edition of the Governor General's Literary Award finalist *Blue Marrow*.

"I refuse to forget

their stories, their laughter, their tears."

Holy Eucharist

On the Rez are the rectories of the priest and nuns.
Next door are the mud-straw-plastered log shacks
of the churchgoers.
The priest reverently lifts
a starch-white invocation of the dead,
pastes it on the kneeling tongues.

In residential school, after choking out the night's soul
in the confessional, the children line up.
Their lashed tongues receive the crucified man.

On the Rez the maggots feast
on the bones of our mothers, fathers,
brothers, sisters, aunts, uncles, cousins,
grandfathers, grandmothers.
All these exhausted ancestors,
lives taken by rope, gun, knives, axe,
heroin, cocaine, fire, beer, whiskey, wine,
cancer, tuberculosis, small pox.
All this swallowing, this inheritance we've
ingested from the body of christ
since October 1492.

I refuse to forget
their stories, their laughter, their tears.
I refuse to forget
the stern discipline of their teachings.
Lakes still filled with our weeping
at each gravesite.

My body is covered with this self-flagellation
of the crucifix that lays on its side.

miyo kisikaw

The cry is not so far away, just a few steps downward
to the guest room, he hasn't slept very long
short intervals of sleep so afraid he will miss out.
His small hands thump whatever is in his reach
as if conducting the house of parliament
he demands that we pay attention.

This evening I walked through rain-soaked grass
stole eighteen eggs right from the grackle's
beady eyes. She scolded me as if I was ripping
her heart out. Those
song birds are missing though the occasional
Baltimore oriole sings from the trees.
I miss the chortling sympathy from the wild.

He sings to his mother's breast
hiccup songs of anticipation as the flow of
translucent white flows from the nipples.
It gushes as he sucks, so greedy with want.
He lets go, bends backward to survey the room
lifts his trunkish body, grabs his mother's chest
small mouth plastered against her frontier.

I should, I suppose, mourn for the unborn
chicks, but I rationalize the prairie is dry
without the symphony of the song birds.
His little chortling, the pick-me-up cry
is harnessed to my heart,
my grandson, my prairie melody.

Educator Connections

Read the editors' thoughts and engage in reflection. Respond to the questions that follow on your own or with your colleague(s).

PERSONAL CONNECTIONS

Christine: I found Louise Bernice Halfe's poems to be in stark contrast to one another. "Holy Eucharist" is a haunting poem that takes us to the past and exposes the deadly indoctrination of Indigenous children, families, and whole communities, leading even the dead to remain exhausted and unable to go home. Halfe embraces resistance when she states, "I refuse to forget." In contrast, "miyo kisikaw" is about her grandson, whom she refers to as her "prairie melody." This poem gave me a sense of relief after reading "Holy Eucharist," as instead of being about our ancestors who suffered at the hands of the church (and state), the main character in this poem is the next generation, who will not suffer the same fate.

Katya: I had a visceral reaction after reading these poems. I carried them around with me for days and needed to come back to the ideas in them multiple times. As someone who attends church and participates in both religious and spiritual practices, this pushes me into an uncomfortable zone—questioning, feeling uneasy, wondering how to balance old and new beliefs with a critical stance. Whatever discomfort I feel is abstract. The horrific realities experienced at residential schools and their ongoing legacy make me question: How did religious leaders stray so far from the values they purport to represent? I read this during a time when thousands of unmarked and unnamed graves of children were discovered. I think these poems speak to the processes of decolonization that are necessary, and how embedded colonial thinking is with many Christian religions. "Holy Eucharist" reminds me of how reconciliation shouldn't be easy. It reveals the entanglement that exists with past and present educational systems. How do educational systems regain the trust of Indigenous communities?

EDUCATOR INQUIRY AND ACTIONS

- How are you personally and professionally connected (or disconnected) from these poems?

- How does "Holy Eucharist" demonstrate resistance? What is being resisted?

- Reflect on your participation in the National Day for Truth and Reconciliation as a school team. Have each team member share what they have done to raise awareness of important truths about residential schools in their classroom. What could be done better? What do you need to learn more about, or what resources do you need, to teach the topic of residential schools with your students? Make a plan as a schoolwide team to ensure that this moves beyond a one-day event.

- Reflect on the terms *decolonization* and *Indigenization*. What do these mean to your educational context?

- How might memories and the refusal to forget form part of a process of decolonization?

- Generate a list of ways you are responding to the Truth and Reconciliation Commission's Calls to Action.[1] If the list is short, make a plan to become familiar with the Calls to Action and collaborate with colleagues to investigate actions you can take in response to one of them.

- If you are teaching in a private or religious-based school setting, what do these poems teach you about harms of the past and reconciliation? What work does your organization still need to do?

---

[1] Truth and Reconciliation Commission of Canada, *Truth and Reconciliation Commission of Canada: Calls to Action* (2015), publications.gc.ca/collections/collection_2015/trc/IR4 -8-2015-eng.pdf.

Classroom Connections

Introduce to students the poems and the Connected Concepts you wish to focus on. Use the following questions, prompts, and resource suggestions to guide student learning.

CONNECTED CONCEPTS

- Residential schools

- Decolonization

- Truth and reconciliation

CONNECTING TO SELF: PROMPTS FOR PERSONAL REFLECTION

Beginning

- What were residential schools? Why were they created?

- How do you think the children who attended residential school felt?

- How do you feel after reading these pieces? Did you feel personally connected to (or disconnected from) these poems?

Bridging

- What is the mood of "Holy Eucharist" and how do you know?

- In "Holy Eucharist," what is being resisted?

- What might Indigenization look like, sound like, and feel like?

Beyond

- What is being juxtaposed in "Holy Eucharist"?

- How is figurative language used within the poems and what meanings does it convey?

- What is Halfe describing in "miyo kisikaw"?

❭ **Beginning**

- Share a time when you felt powerless. Share a time when you felt powerful.

- Share your interpretation of or response to each of these poems, and discuss how they were similar or different.

❭ **Bridging**

- Share your physical, emotional, mental, and spiritual reactions to these poems.

- Discuss ways to move beyond a feel-good approach to reconciliation.

● **Beyond**

- Share your understandings of decolonization or Indigenization.

- Discuss what these poems demonstrate about resistance, both individually and as a pair of texts.

TALKING BACK

"Holy Eucharist" reveals the horrifying realities surrounding residential schools and demonstrates resistance and a poetic talking back, in a Survivor's words, to religious and colonial systems and structures.

- **Problem exposing:** As a class, respond to the harms of past educational policy by revising your school's land acknowledgment to take into account your learning. Does the acknowledgment address the intergenerational effects of residential schools? If so, how?

- **Juxtaposing:** Read and engage with both "Holy Eucharist" and "miyo kisikaw." What does this reveal? Pair these alongside Nicola Campbell's poems (pages 176–177) and juxtapose the feelings and ideas that surface in-between.

⟩ **Beginning**

- What do you still need to learn about residential schools? Think of a big question and use this question to guide your investigation of Orange Shirt Day resources.

⟩ **Bridging**

- In the summer of 2021, news of thousands of unmarked graves of Indigenous children at former residential schools was reported across Canada. As a class, use your voice to creatively respond to this atrocity. Respond to the Truth and Reconciliation Commission's Calls to Action 71 to 76: Missing Children and Burial Information.[2]

⬤ **Beyond**

- What was the role of many churches and religious groups in Indian residential schools? Refer to the published findings of the Truth and Reconciliation Commission. Consider picking a particular religious sect or specific question to guide your inquiry.

- Research one of the residential school sites where unmarked graves were discovered. How might you respond and share what you have learned with a new audience? What are the next steps for your own research? Inquire into a site that has not yet been searched—how might you support the call for it to be searched?

---

2   Available at <publications.gc.ca/collections/collection_2015/trc/IR4-8-2015-eng.pdf>.

Books

When We Were Alone, by David A. Robertson (HighWater Press, 2016; ages 6–8/grades K–2).
This gentle book can be used to begin discussions around residential schools with young children.

Amik Loves School: A Story of Wisdom, by Katherena Vermette (HighWater Press, 2015; ages 3–5/grades K–2).
In this story, a young boy learns that his grandfather attended residential school and invites him to see how his school experience differs.

I Lost My Talk, by Rita Joe, and *I'm Finding My Talk*, by Rebecca Thomas (Nimbus Publishing, 2021; ages 4–8/grades K–3).
Mi'kmaw Elder Rita Joe's poem, inspired by her experience at the Shubenacadie Residential School, reveals the pain of losing her language and voice and celebrates the survival of her culture. Rebecca Thomas's companion poem depicts the experience of being part of the generation of children of residential school Survivors.

The Orange Shirt Story, by Phyllis Webstad (Medicine Wheel Education, 2018; ages 6–10/grades 1–5).
This book tells the story of the author's first day of residential school, when her orange shirt—a gift from her granny—was taken from her and never returned. Webstad's story inspired the entire country to honour residential school Survivors by wearing orange shirts on September 30, now officially recognized as the National Day for Truth and Reconciliation.

Reflections From Them Days: A Residential School Memoir From Nunatsiavut, by Nellie Winters (Inhabit Education, 2020; ages 11–14/grades 6–9).
In this book, the author, a respected Elder, Knowledge Holder, and artisan, recounts her life as a child with her family in Okak Bay, and her experiences after being forced to attend residential school far from her home.

Sugar Falls, by David A. Robertson (HighWater Press, 2012; ages 15–18/ grades 9–12).

This graphic novel is based on the true story of Betty Ross, Elder from Cross Lake First Nation. In this book, the Elder shares her experiences at residential school and demonstrates her resilience, strength, and determination to survive.

Online

KAIROS Blanket Exercise, KAIROS. <www.kairosblanketexercise.org>.

This exercise, presented in collaboration with Indigenous Elders and educators, is an interactive lesson that shows history from an Indigenous perspective with the intention of fostering reconciliation.

PART TWO

RESILIENCE

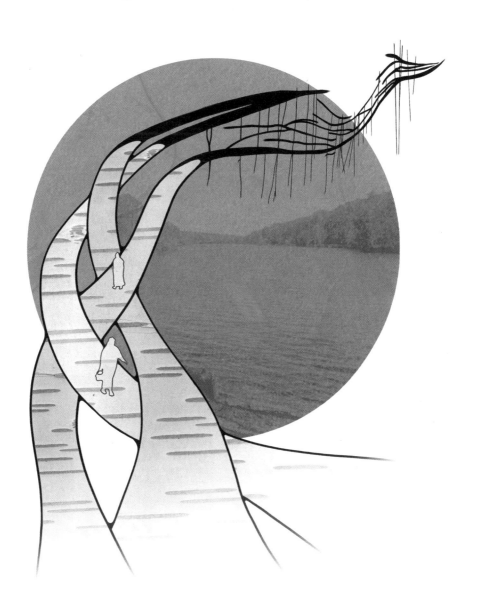

PART 2: RESILIENCE addresses important and often overlooked topics that connect to mental, physical, emotional, and spiritual health and well-being. David Robertson and Wanda John-Kehewin's pieces look at mental health and the power of writing. KC Adams and Lisa Boivin each invite you into their artistic practice, showing how visual mediums support personal and community resilience through activism that breathes new life into important topics.

After reading the narratives and poems in part 1, you may need some time and space to reflect before working with the texts in this section. Reflect on what you are feeling and thinking. What supports do you need to engage further with the topic of resurgence? What supports might your students need? We encourage you to check in with your students before connecting with the voices and perspectives presented in part 2.

There is an openness and rawness to the work the authors and artists in this book present to you as a reader. Treat each text and the voice of the contributor with **respect**, and model for your students how to do so.[1] Consider that David Robertson and Wanda John-Kehewin are sharing stories of their own struggles and giving you a window into their life experiences. Honour the bravery and vulnerability that is needed to share one's struggles openly. Before you read, consider what you need to learn more about to engage with the topic of mental health with students—and consider how you maintain your own health and well-being.

---

1   In each part overview, we focus on four of Indigenous scholar Dr. Jo-ann Archibald Q'um Q'um Xiiem's (Stó:lō and St'át'imc) storywork principles for becoming story-ready: respect, responsibility, reverence, and reciprocity. See Part Overviews: Becoming Story-Ready on page 7 for a description of these principles.

Lisa Boivin's contribution calls on readers to take **responsibility** for learning more about "Canada's shameful history of sterilizing Indigenous women" before engaging with this difficult topic.[2] What do you still need to learn to address issues of systemic racism in your educational context? While the topic of sterilization is not appropriate for younger learners, the underlying topics of body image, body sovereignty, and the ethics of consent can be used to reframe the focus of Boivin's work for your students.

The knowledge within KC Adams's visual contributions is layered and complex. Have **reverence** for these creations as powerful storytelling tools. In her artist's statement, Adams shares how her artistic practice is supporting the creation of her own knowledge bundle. When viewing her pieces, consider how we listen differently to an art piece than a written work, and encourage students to do the same. Consider both the artistic product and the process. You may want to look at elements of art to interpret the pieces (for example, lines, colour, shape, and use of space), and consider how Adams's worldview and Cree/Ojibway perspective factor into the meaning and process.

Consider the principle of **reciprocity** as you learn about resilience in this section. How can you ensure that creative and inspiring stories of Indigenous resilience are given back to the community? How can you extend this to your students and encourage them to share what they are learning?

---

2   Erika Dyck, "Canada's Shameful History of Sterilizing Indigenous Women," *The Conversation*, December 7, 2018, www.indianz.com/News/2018/12/07/erika-dyck-canadas -shameful-history-of-s.asp.

"I was sure that nobody could understand what I was going through; nobody could feel what I felt. It turns out I was wrong."

"Seen in a Good Way":
Reading and Writing Through
Mental Health Struggles

DAVID A. ROBERTSON (he/him/his), a member of Norway House Cree Nation, is the 2021 recipient of the Writer's Union of Canada's Freedom to Read Award. He is the author of more than 25 books for young readers including *When We Were Alone*, which won a Governor General's Literary Award, The Reckoner trilogy, and the memoir *Black Water: Family, Legacy, and Blood Memory*. He is writer and host of the podcast *Kíwew*, which won the 2021 RTDNA Prairie Region Award for Best Podcast.

ORRY IS NOTHING new to me; I've just started to write about it and talk about it. I've lived with anxiety my entire life. When I was younger, I couldn't put a name to it. I knew what I was thinking and feeling, but that was it. I used to have these feelings at night, where I understood my insignificance—the size of me compared to the endlessness of space, my lifespan pitted against eternity. I'd pace around the house feeling like a molecule, and it would take me hours to fall back asleep. I used to worry about death. When I developed a heart condition in high school, that worry became even more real. Though I eventually underwent a procedure that fixed my heart, the fear stayed, and to my knowledge, there is no procedure to fix anxiety. So, I've carried it with me.

Ten years ago, I had a nervous breakdown and didn't think I'd ever get out of it. The weight of my anxiety was a boulder. I refused to do anything but the bare minimum: Work my day job, eat three meals. Other than that, I spent time on the couch or in bed, certain that if I tried to walk across the hall, I'd die. One evening, my wife told me to get groceries, and I said I couldn't. I'd collapse in the middle of the grocery store, and that would be that. My wife asked me, "If you think you're dying, how do you want to live your last days?" So, I went grocery shopping. I didn't die. And amazingly, on the way home, I felt better than I'd felt in months.

I was not cured. There is no cure for anxiety. But this was the beginning of how I learned to cope with it. I did things even when my anxiety told me that I couldn't. (I talk about my anxiety as though it's an entity, and in many ways, it is.) I started to see a psychiatrist. I went to group therapy sessions. That's when I realized more people felt like me. Before that, I was sure that nobody could understand what I was going through; nobody could feel what I felt. It turns out I was wrong. And once again, this realization made me feel better. Not *better*, but more like myself. Empowered.

I'd never been public about my anxiety. I dealt with it, or didn't, privately, within the confines of my family. But I started to speak publicly about it in the many lectures, presentations, keynotes, and interviews I do. I began to write about it as well, most notably in my young adult supernatural murder-mystery trilogy, The Reckoner. I created a character named Cole, a thinly veiled version of myself. While I don't have superpowers as Cole does, I do have similar mental health struggles. His anxiety feels the same way as mine often does. His panic attacks feel the same way as mine can. The way his mind affects his body is the way my mind affects my body. And despite all the anxiety, he finds a way to be a hero. That was my message to both myself and readers: You can live with anxiety. You can do incredible things. Sure, you may not be able to bend metal bars, but sometimes something as simple as going grocery shopping is a heroic act, and that makes you feel powerful like you are leaping over a building.

This amazing thing started to happen. Whenever I did readings from The Reckoner, from any of the three books in the trilogy, at least one person from the audience came up to me after and told me they were going through what Cole was going through. Or I'd get a private message from somebody who'd read *Monsters* (the second book in the series), just to tell me that they felt *seen* in a good way, that reading about Cole helped them heal. It's helped me heal, too.

The Reckoner Rises, the graphic novel series that acts as a sequel to The Reckoner trilogy, is a continuation of that intent to share mental health struggles authentically so that people who are struggling can continue to feel seen. This includes Indigenous youth living with mental health issues at a disproportionate rate compared to the rest of Canada. I thought maybe, in the smallest way, I could continue to help by sharing my struggles through Cole's character. And now, I'm doing so in a medium that lends itself, more than any other form of literature, to the sort of engagement that leads to retention and learning—the visual medium of the graphic novel. Now, not only can readers experience Cole's story, his struggles, and his victories over those struggles, but they can also see them. And through him, continue to be seen. They can see him do breathing exercises. They can see him talk to his psychiatrist and have a conversation that I've had with my mental health professional. They can watch him smudge with his friend to cleanse his body and mind. They can watch him fall down and get back up. And they'll realize that, like Cole, when they fall they can get back up.

If people have fun reading Cole's continuing story in The Reckoner Rises, including its first book, *Breakdown*, great. I want it to be fun. It has to be fun. If that's all they get, I'm okay with that. But if even one person looks at Cole and sees themselves reflected in some way, either because they are Indigenous like him, or struggling like him, then I think I'll sleep a lot better than I did when I was a kid, feeling so small. Because I'm not, and neither are you, and we're in this together.

Page from The Reckoner Rises, Volume 1: *Breakdown*, by David A. Robertson, illustrated by Scott B. Henderson and Donovan Yaciuk.

Educator Connections

Read the editors' thoughts and engage in reflection. Respond to the questions that follow on your own or with your colleague(s).

PERSONAL CONNECTIONS

Christine: For me, this piece reinforces how stories can be used as tools to empower students to talk about what they're feeling and ultimately build resiliency. I am reminded of the importance of representation in stories and how life saving stories can be. I wonder how I can better foster positive mental health and mental health education in my classroom.

Katya: I am learning about David Robertson's inner strength. I hear about the importance of seeing yourself in literature, and I know many teachers are working at improving Indigenous representation in their school and classroom libraries, but Robertson actually shows how it has helped him heal. His courage to be vulnerable in sharing his struggles offers a rawness but also a reality that invites us to share and make deep connections.

EDUCATOR INQUIRY AND ACTIONS

- What does reading about David Robertson's experience of managing his anxiety teach you?

- In your various roles, what do you do to support your own mental health and wellness? How might these practices be embedded in your professional life and work in the classroom?

- How can you support mental health literacy and education and reduce stigma in your current teaching context?

- How does this piece relate to resilience? How can we teach students to be resilient in everyday situations?

- Take time to search out mental health services that are available for students, parents, and caregivers in your local area. What can you do as a school community to support and take care of community members? Brainstorm ways to involve parents, offer community networking events, and provide valuable social roles within the school.

Classroom Connections

Introduce to students the narrative and the Connected Concepts you wish to focus on. Use the following questions, prompts, and resource suggestions to guide student learning.

CONNECTED CONCEPTS

- Feelings

- Representation

- Mental health

- Resilience

CONNECTING TO SELF: PROMPTS FOR PERSONAL REFLECTION

Beginning

- What makes you feel small or, as David Robertson says, "like a molecule"?

- Who or what helps you feel better when you are anxious or sad?

Bridging

- What do you carry with you that no one sees?

- Have you ever encountered a character in a book that made you feel *seen*? Or who had overcome challenges similar to your own?

- **Beyond**
  - Do you know where to go to access mental health resources?
  - What does it mean to "be resilient"? How can we learn to be resilient?

CONNECTING TO COMMUNITY: PROMPTS FOR LEARNING CIRCLES

- **Beginning**
  - Pick a feeling and share a story from your life when you felt that way.
  - Share how you take care of your mind, heart, and spirit.

- **Bridging**
  - Share a time when you "felt seen in a good way."
  - Share a story of a time when someone supported you when you were feeling low.

- **Beyond**
  - Discuss the meaning of resilience.
  - Share a story of resilience.

TALKING BACK

This personal essay reflects how David Robertson has used writing as a medium to talk back to his own feelings and challenges. He is also talking back to a system that has under-represented Indigenous people in books. His work has supported changing this and empowering Indigenous youth.

- **Problem exposing:** Our feelings—that no one sees—influence our mental, physical, emotional, and spiritual health and well-being. Find ways to talk back to those unhealthy internal feelings that make you feel small, "like a molecule." One way of talking back is to write affirming statements to yourself and to one another.

- **Juxtaposing:** Explore the layered nature of identity and the idea that people's perceptions can be biased and damaging. Seeking inspiration from KC Adams's book *Perception* or her photo series of the same name, discuss identities and stigma. Create your own photos and captions of yourself and your classmates that juxtapose perceptions and reality.

INQUIRY

⟩ Beginning

- Look at your classroom library. Do you see yourself represented in the books? What stories are being told? Whose experiences and cultures are missing? How can seeing representations of characters you identify with or people who have endured similar challenges contribute to a positive sense of self?

⟩ Bridging

- Create a visual representation of yourself that illustrates a struggle or challenge. How is the colour or medium used to show feelings and emotions? Create an artist's statement that discusses how you showed resilience in your work.

- How is writing and representation an act of resistance? How can you use the process of writing as a mental health strategy?

⟩ Beyond

- What resources support mental health and well-being in your area? Share this information within your school community or online/on social media so other students know where to access these supports.

- How do people become resilient? Find an online video about someone's journey overcoming hardship.

- What is a mental health plan and how can you create one? Develop an individualized plan for "bouncing back" after facing hardship.

Books

My Heart Fills With Happiness, by Monique Gray Smith (Orca Books, 2016; ages 1–5/grades preK–K).
This board book, written to support the wellness of Indigenous children and their families, asks young readers to think about what makes them happy, celebrating the moments that bring them joy. (Also available in French: *J'ai le coeur rempli de bonheur.*)

Trudy's Healing Stone, by Trudy Spiller (Medicine Wheel Education, 2019; ages 4–6/grades K–1).
This book tells the story of a girl who learns to deal with difficult emotions with the help of Mother Earth.

The Reckoner trilogy, by David A. Robertson (HighWater Press, 2017–2019; ages 15–18/grades 9–12).
The books in this acclaimed young adult novel series (*Strangers*, *Monsters*, and *Ghosts*) follow Cole Harper as he returns to his community of Wounded Sky First Nation, addressing issues such as bullying, trauma, and anxiety.

Perception: A Photo Series, by KC Adams (HighWater Press, 2019).
This book visually juxtaposes Indigenous stereotypes with images of realities and strengths. Each pair of photos provides rich provocations for discussion.

Online

Circle of Courage poster and philosophy, Reclaiming Youth Network (2007). <www.edu.gov.mb.ca/k12/cur/cardev/gr9_found/courage_poster.pdf>.
This curricular poster visually summarizes the Circle of Courage, a model of positive youth development first described in the book *Reclaiming Youth at Risk*. The model is based on four values all children need for growth: belonging, mastery, independence, and generosity.

"The very act of sharing the traumas and being open about them releases the shame we carry around like buckets of water, trying so hard not to spill anything."

Writing as a Therapeutic Medium

WANDA JOHN-KEHEWIN (she/her/hers) is a Cree writer who uses writing as a therapeutic medium through which to understand and respond to the near decimation of First Nations cultures, languages, and traditions. She has written two books of poetry, *In the Dog House* and *Seven Sacred Truths*, as well as two books for children. She is currently in her first year of her Master of Fine Arts at the University of British Columbia.

READING AND WRITING have always been a form of escape from the dysfunctional world happening around me on the reserve, especially when I was a child; they are also a way for me to make sense of the world as an adult. Writing is a way to create and build worlds that no one else has control over but me; such an act of free expression was empowering for a child used to feeling powerless, hopeless, and helpless. The other half of the survival equation was that I had teachers in my life who validated me and regarded my writing as worthy enough to be out in the world. I could have a voice, even if it was on paper. I have had many teachers in my life who encouraged me and saw beyond the trauma and created space for me to grow beyond the pain of my past.

Just how important are our educators and mentors? Very important to children struggling with dysfunction, negative self-identity, and low self-esteem. It is important to remember that these struggles are happening all over the world, not just on reserves. Educators and mentors are very important to children's lives, especially those children who come from trauma. Educators and mentors can help children see a way out of powerlessness, hopelessness, and helplessness—a way to escape into the worlds they create through writing and the arts.

This whole idea of educators and mentors being there to help nurture individuals beyond a limited worldview of dysfunction applies to adults as well; no one is ever too old to get into the arts, even if you only use it as a way to process pain. Writing and art allow us to process our trauma and give us ways to understand it. If we understood it all at once, it might be too much to handle, but the act of expressing ourselves through art and writing can help us break it down into manageable steps. One example would be my very first book of poetry, *In the Dog House*, which was written during a two-year depression and helped me process some of my complex trauma.

I have taken a few workshops about trauma and read a few books about it, but not enough to slap a sign on my door and open up for business; I can only draw on personal experience when I describe how writing has been therapeutic and how it has saved me.

There is something freeing about standing in my truth, writing about the traumas of the past, and sharing that truth. That is not my truth alone, but my grandmother's, my mother's, my dad's, and the truth of many other Indigenous people because of colonialism and its systems. Writing is me deciding not to carry trauma around anymore and releasing it into the world in hopes that it will reach others. The very act of sharing the traumas and being open about them releases the shame we carry around like buckets of water, trying so hard not to spill anything.

I wrote a piece called "A Letter to My Nine-Year-Old-Self" that is about thinking about suicide at nine years of age. I cried through the entire process of writing it. I grieved for the nine-year-old that was me, struggling with the dysfunctional world around me. Looking at it through the lens of an adult I was able to see that the fault was not my parents, or grandparents, or family members, but part of a bigger problem called colonization, which is a blanket term at best. The editing process of that piece became less and less painful as I continued to read it aloud and edit it. I know it is such a vulnerable piece that it probably requires a trigger warning, but how many children out there are thinking about suicide and not saying anything about it? How many adults out there live with these thoughts every day and suffer alone?

Writing "A Letter to My Nine-Year-Old Self" helped me process the trauma and dysfunction surrounding my childhood through the lens of my adult self and address these issues with the voice of reflection. The act of thinking, writing, and processing my nine-year-old thoughts as an adult has created space for the hurt nine-year-old to heal and allowed the adult to create space for that pain and accept it as a part of me; not as something to be ashamed of, but something to share so others do not have to feel alone. When we create space for common experience, we create room for healing.

Writing is a therapeutic medium, and by sharing the pain, we can also help others realize that they are not alone. That is one thing I have always felt—alone, thinking that no one could possibly understand what I was going through and that I wasn't good enough and that's why my life was hell and that I would never get out of it. I wanted to reach others who felt alone with the "craziness" that only another person from the same "craziness" could understand.

From the very first time I stood in front of a group of people and read my painful work in 2008 to the last time I did a public reading for students at the University of Alberta over Zoom in 2021, a lot has changed. My evolution is apparent to those who view old YouTube videos of me reading my work with my voice quavering, knees shaking, and tears flowing that I promised myself I would not shed in public. That whole process of standing in my truth has brought me to where I am today—sitting in front of a computer contemplating what I will write next.

On my healing journey of standing in my truth and writing, two books of poetry came out of my need to be heard as an Indigenous woman. I also needed to give my mother a voice and felt a sense of urgency to leave a written record for my children and grandchildren, so that one day they would be able to read about and understand the near decimation of us as Indigenous peoples. How many Indigenous people have died without their voices ever being heard, as if they weren't important enough to be heard? Most of my ancestors died without a voice.

I have much to say and explain before I leave this world. Children don't always realize the questions they will have, not until after their parents pass on like mine did. I want my children to have answers to questions I asked myself only after my parents passed away at age 48 and 51. I want to make sure they know none of this is their fault. I want to tell all Indigenous people—this isn't their fault. What better way to do that than to stand in my truth and publish it for all the world to see, showing I am not ashamed of where I come from, teaching my children the importance of voice.

As the years pass, a lot of the traumatic debris is cleared away, leaving more manageable neural pathways, and my love of writing (beyond a therapeutic medium) shows itself in ways I never would have imagined possible. My nine-year-old self would have been astonished to know about the graphic novel series and young adult novel in my future. I have also written my first film script. These wonders are thanks to another one of those mentors/educators I talk about who are very important to our lives.

Just how far can we go when we are no longer living in survival mode? As far as we can dream...and as far as we are willing to go. If the door is closed, ask for the key. And if there is no key, make one or find another door.

Educator Connections

Read the editors' thoughts and engage in reflection. Respond to the questions that follow on your own or with your colleague(s).

PERSONAL CONNECTIONS

Christine: What an inspiring piece! I appreciate how Wanda John-Kehewin frames writing as an escape, as a coping mechanism. I relate because schoolwork was always an escape for me. I remember getting lost in stories and forgetting about my worries, and this continues to be a coping mechanism for me to this day. As someone who goes to therapy, I've been curious about doing work to heal my inner child, as Wanda John-Kehewin did by writing a letter to her nine-year-old self. I am left wondering how I can encourage students to choose healthy coping mechanisms that work for them and carry them throughout their lives.

Katya: I connect with Wanda John-Kehewin's phrase "the shame we carry around like buckets of water, trying so hard not to spill anything." For many years, I did this. Beginning around the age of nine, I carried the weight of my father's alcoholism, which took hold of all our family members for decades. I am embracing the vulnerability that Wanda encourages; without giving too much information, I do feel a sense of release from typing even that small drop from the bucket onto the page. It's something I still carry with me and am making meaning from. The power of mentors also resonates with me. I think for me hopefulness and a sense of balance amidst traumatic experiences came from having supportive people around me at critical times and creative outlets that gave space to both hurt and to heal.

- How do you encourage students to "stand in their truth"?

- Take time for individual reflection to consider: If you could write a letter to your nine-year-old self, what would you say?

- As an educator, what can you do to support your own mental health and well-being? Who do you need support from? Generate a list of mental health strategies as a school team.

- What "traumatic debris" do you carry with you as a teacher? (As a starting point, you could focus on your teaching practice.) Journal about this and reflect on how it affects your daily and ongoing practice. You may want to keep this private. Instead of showing it to your colleagues, share with them a self-affirming message that *talks back* to what you wrote.

- Discuss the supports in place at your school regarding trauma-informed and responsive practices. Survey older students about related topics they would like to address or need support with. Generate a list of the professional learning you think is still needed. What does this look like in early/middle/senior years?

- Reflect on your current literacy practices and how they nurture students' self-identity and self-esteem. Are you already using "therapeutic mediums" in your class? How can you encourage students to discover their voices (in any multimodal medium)? Share what is working as a school team.

- How have you supported a student's potential and made space for them to grow from traumas or crises? Share a story of someone who has been supportive or has mentored you through past or present challenges. Incorporate what they have taught you into a plan of action for someone in your class who may need it.

Classroom Connections

Introduce to students the narrative and the Connected Concepts you wish to focus on. Use the following questions, prompts, and resource suggestions to guide student learning.

CONNECTED CONCEPTS

- Identity
- Voice
- Escapism and processing trauma

CONNECTING TO SELF: PROMPTS FOR PERSONAL REFLECTION

Beginning
- What makes you feel like you're not alone?
- When do you feel like you want to "escape" something?
- What activities take your mind off your worries?

Bridging
- What has helped shape your identity?
- What forms of "escape" do you use when you are upset? What is the difference between healthy forms of escape and unhealthy forms of escape?

Beyond
- If you could write a letter to your nine-year-old self, what would you say?
- What does the author mean when she says "a limited worldview"?
- What is trauma and how do people overcome it?

CONNECTING TO COMMUNITY: PROMPTS FOR LEARNING CIRCLES

⟩ Beginning

- Share a time when you felt hopeless. Share a time when you felt hopeful.

- Share an activity that takes your mind off your worries.

⟩ Bridging

- Voice your opinion on something you are passionate about.

- Share the name of someone you look up to and describe what makes them a good role model.

- Describe a time when someone you look up to helped you.

● Beyond

- Discuss the role of mentors or positive influences in your life and how they have supported you.

- Describe which medium (for example, writing, video, podcast) you would use to share your own story and explain why you would choose this medium.

TALKING BACK

Wanda John-Kehewin shares how colonial structures have had a negative and generational impact on Indigenous communities. This piece talks back to and exposes these systems of oppression by providing a more central and powerful space for stories/images/works of Indigenous resilience.

- **Problem exposing:** Write an "I am" or "Where I am from" poem.[1] These forms can help you say what you want and need to release, but with the mystery of interpretation providing a safe outlet without the need to elaborate to an audience.

---

1   See, for example, Linda Christensen's "Where I'm From: Inviting Students' Lives Into the Classroom." *Rethinking Schools*, August 6, 2021, rethinkingschools.org/2021/08/06/where-im-from/.

- **Juxtaposing:** Create masks with words and images that show how you feel on the inside, and juxtapose this with words and images that show how you are perceived on the outside.[2]

INQUIRY

> **Beginning**

- What qualities do we look for in supportive people? Create a poster that represents these qualities to display in your classroom.

- How have you been supported/mentored/guided along your journey? Share your reflections in a multimodal format such as a video, map, poem, or collage. This could be created in honour of a person who has supported you.

> **Bridging**

- What are coping strategies and how can they be used to help people deal with life's difficulties? Create a poster that presents coping strategies to display in your classroom or on social media.

- Imagine what a supportive healing space looks and feels like. On a piece of paper or in a digital space, use drawing tools to create a healing space unique to you that offers you what you need to heal.

> **Beyond**

- What can you do to support or raise awareness of suicide prevention? What are the current realities? Consider connecting with another school community to develop positive networks of support.

- What do you care about? Become an activist for this cause. Use your voice like Wanda John-Kehewin and share your learning with your class and beyond.

---

2 For more guidance on the mask activity, see "What Aspects of Our Identities Do We Show to Others?" Facing History & Ourselves, www.facinghistory.org/resource-library/identity-and-community/aspect-identities-show-others. KC Adams's book *Perception* or her photo series of the same name would be a great visual support for this activity.

CONNECTIONS TO INDIGENOUS RESOURCES

Books

Siha Tooskin Knows the Strength of His Hair, by Charlene Bearhead and Wilson Bearhead (HighWater Press, 2020; ages 9–11/grades 3–5).
This book follows the main character, an 11-year-old Nakota boy, as he explores what having strength really means and where to find strength when he needs it.

Surviving the City series, by Tasha Spillett (HighWater Press, 2019–; ages 12–14/grades 7–8).
This graphic novel series follows two friends as they cope with the challenges of growing up in the city and losing a loved one. The books touch on the legacy of colonialism and its impacts on these young women.

April Raintree, by Beatrice Mosionier (HighWater Press, 2016; ages 15–18/grades 9–12).
This novel (revised from the original for young adults) tells the story of two sisters as they grow up separated from each other in the child welfare system, touching on the harsh realities facing Indigenous peoples.

Birch Bark Technology

KC ADAMS (she/her/hers) is an award-winning Cree/Ojibway/British Winnipeg-based artist who works in a wide variety of mediums. KC graduated from Concordia University with a Bachelor of Fine Arts, and her work is in many permanent collections both nationally and internationally, including pieces at the National Gallery of Canada. She is a recent recipient of the Winnipeg Arts Council's Making a Mark Award and the Aboriginal Circle of Educators' Trailblazing Award.

B IRCH BARK TECHNOLOGY and *Water Carrier and Grandmother Moon* are two pieces from my exhibition *Gage'gajiiwaan* (Ojibway word meaning "water flowing eternally brings people together"). The work reflects my learning relationships between land, ancestral knowledge, memory, and the sacredness of water. I used the imagery of birch bark because of its connection to the natural world and technology in making cultural objects: canoes, baskets, shelters, plates, and sunglasses. However, they were more than just utilitarian objects: they held knowledge bundles (traditional teachings) passed on to the next generation.

In *Birch Bark Technology*, I use the image of the morning star to comment on my ancestors' relationship with the stars (upper spirit realm) and how it acts as a guide. The piece *Water Carrier and Grandmother Moon* represents learning about the ancient tradition of clay vessels, and their imagery was about pregnancy (water carrier) and grandmother moon. Learning about my culture, I can reflect through my artistic practice and create my own knowledge bundle about land, waters, life-givers, and water protectors.

"Learning about my culture, I can reflect through my artistic practice and create my own knowledge bundle about land, waters, life-givers, and water protectors."

Birch Bark Technology, by ᴋᴄ Adams.

(Image courtesy of ᴋᴄ Adams.)

Water Carrier and Grandmother Moon, by KC Adams.
(Image courtesy of KC Adams.)

Educator Connections

Read the editors' thoughts and engage in reflection. Respond to the questions that follow on your own or with your colleague(s).

PERSONAL CONNECTIONS

Christine: KC Adams's *Gage'gajiiwaan* exhibit is stunning! I love how she fuses the traditional and the modern: traditional birch bark carvings reflecting an electrical board, signifying how our Indigenous cultures are rooted in tradition but simultaneously ever evolving with the times. I find these images inspiring and a testament to the resilience of Indigenous culture and people. Our knowledge bundles survived the storm of attempted genocide. These pieces are brilliant and my brain is spinning thinking of all the ways they can be used to teach youth about the resilience and beauty of our culture!

Katya: I think KC Adams's work bridges traditional and contemporary teachings in ways that are both restoring and re-storying. My mind goes to both my personal and professional experiences and responsibilities. The piece *Water Carrier and Grandmother Moon* reminds me of the experience of being pregnant when my grandmother passed away. I felt connected to new life within me and I wanted to maintain the bond with my grandmother and the knowledges she carried. I think Adams's art as a knowledge bundle is a powerful idea. I can't help but think about how women continue to go missing. Where I live, we have women's bodies being discovered in rivers—carried by water, a source of life. How do we ensure that women's bodies, spirits, and talents are nurtured and respected so that the knowledges and potential they carry can be shared with future generations?

- Both *Birch Bark Technology* and *Water Carrier and Grandmother Moon* show how Indigenous art can carry traditional knowledge within contemporary mediums, living all at once in the past, present, and future. What are you doing as a teacher to keep local traditional teachings alive? How can you ensure knowledges are not portrayed as static? How do you support their revival?

- Share ideas for giving prominence to Indigenous artwork in your teaching.

- Discuss with colleagues how you are using art to teach about important issues.

- Research Indigenous artifacts and art pieces and respect them as knowledge bundles with traditional teachings embedded within them. What do you learn from the artists' statements that accompany the pieces?

Classroom Connections

Introduce to students the narrative and artwork and the Connected Concepts you wish to focus on. Use the following questions, prompts, and resource suggestions to guide student learning.

CONNECTED CONCEPTS

- Decoding art

- Symbolism in art and Indigenous knowledge

CONNECTING TO SELF: PROMPTS FOR PERSONAL REFLECTION

Beginning

- What do you notice when you look at these pieces?

- What materials do you think KC Adams used to create these pieces?

- What symbols and imagery do you notice in each piece?

Bridging

- What is the connection between the womb and the moon in *Water Carrier and Grandmother Moon*?

- How are our bodies connected to the land, waters, and sky/stars?

- What do these pieces teach us about balance?

Beyond

- How does KC Adams's art demonstrate resistance? Resilience?

- Why do you think KC Adams chose to name her exhibit *Gage'gajiiwaan*, meaning "water flowing eternally brings people together"? How is this idea represented in her art?

- How do you think the art represents Adams's "learning relationships between land, ancestral knowledge, memory, and the sacredness of water"?

CONNECTING TO COMMUNITY: PROMPTS FOR LEARNING CIRCLES

Beginning

- Share your noticings, wonderings, and feelings as you look at *Birch Bark Technology* and *Water Carrier and Grandmother Moon*.

- Share something you like about either *Birch Bark Technology* or *Water Carrier and Grandmother Moon*.

- Share a question you would like to ask KC Adams.

⟩ **Bridging**

- Share what you think these images reveal about the place KC Adams is from.

- Share connections you have with the symbols and imagery in these pieces of art.

● **Beyond**

- Discuss how you think these images were created and what this reveals about Adams's relationship with and knowledge of land.

- Share how these pieces relate to you or your culture.

- Share teachings from your culture about womanhood, menstruation, or pregnancy.

TALKING BACK

KC Adams's pieces *Birch Bark Technology* and *Water Carrier and Grandmother Moon* are beautiful visual representations of how Indigenous cultures are diverse and dynamic. In curriculum, Indigenous cultures may be portrayed as something that existed in the past or as if they are static. What can you do to change this?

- **Problem exposing:** These pieces expose critical issues such as access to water and how the health of water is integrally linked to the health of communities. The description of KC Adams's exhibit *Gage'gajiiwaan* ("water flowing eternally brings people together") states, "In the context of limited access to safe drinking water in too many First Nations communities, calling attention to the inherent sacredness of water is critically important."[1] What can you do to become more aware of water access issues in your local region and call attention to your findings?

---

1   *Gage'gajiiwaan*, Art Gallery of Southwestern Manitoba, agsm.ca/gage'gajiiwaan.

- **Juxtaposing:** Look up KC Adams's full *Gage'gajiiwaan* exhibit and juxtapose it with the "classical" Canadian art created by Cornelius Krieghoff or the Group of Seven. What do you notice? What stands out? What do you wonder?

INQUIRY

⟩ Beginning

- How is birch bark used as a form of technology? Look into scientific and historical perspectives on how the birch tree has been used and how its uses have changed over time. Do some research on your own and then reach out to your local gallery or museum curator for more information.

- What are the stories and significance of the birch tree in Cree and Ojibway cultures?

- Research the tradition of birch bark biting art. Which nation did this tradition originate from? How are the designs created? What do the designs mean? Create a presentation to teach the class about this art form.

⟩ Bridging

- Look into the symbol and significance of the star and the moon in Ojibway and Cree cultures.

- Learn more about the powerful work of Indigenous women artists (such as Ruth Cuthand and Rebecca Belmore). How do other Indigenous women artists represent their knowledges by fusing traditional and contemporary teachings and mediums?

- Research an Indigenous artist who uses a traditional art form (for example, embroidery, quillwork, beading, Inuit soapstone carving) and describe its cultural significance. How is the artist's approach similar to or different than KC Adams's?

- Look at *Birch Bark Technology* and *Water Carrier and Grandmother Moon* through various lenses (such as historical, ecological, biological, and literary) to generate several inquiry questions. Pick one of the questions to investigate further. Draw on resources created by Cree or Ojibway people to help focus the inquiry.

- Explore the ways in which Indigenous culture has changed, adapted, and evolved over time. Challenge yourself to share your learning in a visual format or using a form of technology that is new to you.

CONNECTIONS TO INDIGENOUS RESOURCES

Books

We Are Water Protectors, by Carole Lindstrom (Roaring Brook Press, 2020; ages 3–6/grades preK–1).
This picture book highlights Indigenous efforts to protect the sacredness and safety of water.

Siha Tooskin Knows the Gifts of His People, by Charlene Bearhead and Wilson Bearhead (HighWater Press, 2020; ages 9–11/grades 3–5).
In this book, an 11-year-old Nakota boy learns about Indigenous technology and innovations.

Online

Gage'gajiiwaan exhibit, by KC Adams. <agsm.ca/gage'gajiiwaan>.
Birch Bark Technology and *Water Carrier and Grandmother Moon* were originally featured in this solo exhibit. This resource supports learning more about KC Adams's art and activism. A virtual tour of the exhibit is also available: <kcadams.net/gagegajiiwaan/>.

"One Sky, Many Astronomies," by Wilfred Buck, University of Victoria Astronomy Research Centre, February 9, 2021. <www.uvic.ca/research/centres/arc/home/home/news/wilfred-buck-talk-2021.php>.
In this public talk, Indigenous star lore expert Wilfred Buck shares interconnections between star stories and their significance to Cree cultures and traditions.

"A Short History of Indigenous Blankets in Canada," CBC *Unreserved*, September 6, 2019. <www.cbc.ca/radio/unreserved/uncovering-the -complicated-history-of-blankets-in-indigenous-communities-1.5264926 /a-short-history-of-indigenous-blankets-in-canada-1.5270362>.
From Hudson Bay point blankets to button blankets and star quilts, this segment of *Unreserved* explores the history of blankets in Indigenous communities.

"Colonialism attempted to

blot us out yet here we are."

Images and Health

LISA BOIVIN is a member of the Deninu Kue First Nation and the author/artist of two illustrated books, *We Dream Medicine Dreams* (shortlisted for the 2022 Rocky Mountain Book Award) and *I Will See You Again* (AICL's Best Books of 2020, nominated for First Nation Communities READ Award). She is an interdisciplinary artist and a PhD candidate at the Rehabilitation Sciences Institute at the University of Toronto's Faculty of Medicine.

———————

IMAGES ARE A pedagogical strategy to educate clinicians and health care educators about the impact of Canada's colonial history on health outcomes of Indigenous people and populations. Through my own research journey, I have read thousands of articles and very few inform my practice today. I learned that images have staying power. They occupy a different space in my mind. Images are dynamic; they hang around in my intellectual space and I return periodically to re-examine them and learn different lessons.

Although my images reveal stark colonial realities that weigh heavily on Indigenous bodies, they also illuminate our resilience. It took me a while to figure out that the very composition of the images is a metaphor for our strength as Indigenous people. I start with a black canvas. Those of us who paint are aware that black is the most aggressive colour on the palette. It has the ability to blot out everything. This black represents the dark history of colonialism and how it weighs on the shoulders of Indigenous people. Colonialism attempted to blot us out yet here we are. That is why I paint the bright flowers and the strawberries on the black canvas. I surround our Indigenous bodies with flowers and strawberries because they are as bright and beautiful as we are as Indigenous people.

The following images were commissioned by Senator Yvonne Boyer. They are used as educational tools to create awareness about coerced sterilization in Indigenous women.

The Most Sacred Ceremony, by Lisa Boivin.
"The clipboard represents the process of informed consent. Informed consent is the most sacred ceremony between clinician and patient. This is a ceremony where both parties come together equally and participate in a clinical plan that benefits the patient. As such, I have added a blue jay because they are careful and clear in their communication. Committed to truthfulness and justice, they sing the sweetest songs, encouraging us to move forward in a good way. Clinicians must develop equal relationships with their patients that are free from coercion, with a solid process of informed consent."
(Image and description courtesy of Lisa Boivin.)

The Warning, by Lisa Boivin.

"This is an image of a woman's surgical sterilization. Blue jays are protectors; they swarm around her anesthetized body singing a song of warning. They are telling her she will soon be separated from her biological fertility. However, even this violent act will not sever her from the beauty and resilience of living in her body, which is represented by the flowers and berries growing from her powerful womb."

(Image and description courtesy of Lisa Boivin.)

Educator Connections

Read the editors' thoughts and engage in reflection. Respond to the questions that follow on your own or with your colleague(s).

PERSONAL REFLECTIONS

Christine: While engaging with this piece, I felt sick to my stomach, yet inspired. Lisa Boivin's art juxtaposes the aggressiveness of colonialism with lively scenes of resilience. I am reminded of all the horrors my ancestors experienced at the hands of colonizers through various institutions, including the education, justice, and health care systems. I am forced to ask myself: Are these institutions safe for us today?

Katya: After reading Lisa Boivin's writing, I was left feeling nauseous. I didn't realize the extent to which sterilization was occurring and that it was still happening within the last five years. It made me think of my own children; even though they are very young, I need to teach them more about consent. I think there is a lot of work to do in schools so that this violence ends. These beautiful images are great teachers. They also convey a sense of healing. They tell a story of truth and resiliency—giving visual advice for reconciliation.

EDUCATOR INQUIRY AND ACTIONS

- Lisa Boivin states, "Images are a pedagogical strategy to educate clinicians and health care educators about the impact of Canada's colonial history on health outcomes of Indigenous people and populations." Consider how you use images in the classroom. How might you use visual pedagogical tools to help your learning as a member of a professional learning community have more "staying power"?

- Discuss with your colleagues your approach to teaching ideas around personal safety, consent, and body sovereignty at your grade level. Share ideas, resources, tensions, and insights.

- Discuss the image *The Most Sacred Ceremony* and the power dynamics between clinician/medical professional and patient. How does this connect to power dynamics within schools? How might you reimagine a more balanced relationship between principals, teachers, students, and families?

- Think critically about current school policies and procedures, particularly in relation to attendance policies connected to the involvement of child welfare agencies. To what extent are separations still happening as children are removed from their families and placed in child welfare systems? Inquire into your local statistics and reports.

- As a school team, how do you connect to the Truth and Reconciliation Commission's Calls to Action or the National Inquiry into Missing and Murdered Indigenous Women and Girls' Calls for Justice?[1] Take time to read and engage with the Calls to Action and Calls for Justice, and explore resources such as those provided here in the Connections to Indigenous Resources.

Classroom Connections

Introduce to students the narrative and artwork and the Connected Concepts you wish to focus on. Use the following questions, prompts, and resource suggestions to guide student learning.

CONNECTED CONCEPTS

- Body sovereignty

- Consent

- Systemic racism

---

1   Available at <publications.gc.ca/collections/collection_2015/trc/IR4-8-2015-eng.pdf> and <www.mmiwg-ffada.ca/wp-content/uploads/2019/06/Calls_for_Justice.pdf>.

CONNECTING TO SELF: PROMPTS FOR PERSONAL REFLECTION

Beginning

- What do you think, notice, and wonder when you look at Lisa Boivin's images?

- How do you show respect for yourself and your body?

Bridging

- What is consent? How can we ask for consent? How can we give it?

- What is an appropriate response when someone doesn't give us their consent?

- What is body sovereignty and how can we exercise it?

Beyond

- What is systemic racism?

- What is informed consent?

- What message is Lisa Boivin trying to convey through her images?

CONNECTING TO COMMUNITY: PROMPTS FOR LEARNING CIRCLES

Beginning

- Explain if your preference is to look at art or read a written text and why.

- Discuss how artists can share a story through a drawing or painting.

- Discuss what emotions different colours can represent.

Bridging

- Discuss the power of images in your daily life.

- Describe what consent looks like, sounds like, and feels like.

Beyond

- In her statement, Lisa Boivin says, "images have staying power." Share some images that have stayed with you.

- Discuss the image *The Most Sacred Ceremony* and the power dynamics between clinician/medical professional and patient.

- Discuss the concept of body sovereignty.

TALKING BACK

Lisa Boivin talks back by displaying bright colours and Indigenous imagery to send a message of resilience against colonialism, which is represented as the black background.

- **Problem exposing:** These images are about how people have abused power over Indigenous people and their bodies. Although Boivin focuses on the abuses perpetrated by the health care system, these cannot be separated from the harms done by the judicial, child welfare, and education systems. Have the abuses and unequal treatment stopped, or been renamed, reformulated, and repackaged as something else? In what ways does the education system perpetuate narratives of white supremacy?

- **Juxtaposing:** Juxtapose Lisa Boivin's images with the CTV News article "Tackling Anti-Black Racism in Canadian Health Care."[2] How can we use Lisa Boivin's art as a springboard for discussing anti-Black racism in the medical field?

   Juxtapose Lisa Boivin's art with the APTN News article "Indigenous Nurse and Birth Worker Advocates for More Access to Traditional Support" about the resurgence of traditional Indigenous birthing practices.[3] How does the resurgence of these traditional practices talk back to racist practices of forced sterilization?

---

2   Alexandra Mae Jones, October 6, 2021, www.ctvnews.ca/health/tackling-anti-black-racism-in-canadian-health-care-experts-putting-together-first-primer-of-its-kind-1.5613938.

3   Odette Auger, November 13, 2020, www.aptnnews.ca/national-news/indigenous-nurse-and-birth-worker-advocates-for-more-access-to-traditional-support/.

❯ Beginning

- What rights do children have? Develop a kid-friendly version of the rights of children outlined in the United Nations Convention on the Rights of the Child.[4]

- What rights do Indigenous peoples have? Develop a kid-friendly version of the rights of Indigenous peoples outlined in the United Nations Declaration on the Rights of Indigenous Peoples.[5]

❯ Bridging

- What is systemic racism? Research an example of systemic racism in Canada and present it to your class, outlining what was done and what still needs to be done to prevent this from happening again.

❯ Beyond

- Why are there so many missing and murdered Indigenous women and girls in Canada? Read the Executive Summary of *Reclaiming Power and Place: The Final Report of the National Inquiry into Missing and Murdered Indigenous Women and Girls* and summarize your findings for the class.[6]

- Select a news story highlighting an example of racism in the health care system in Canada. Create a case study to share with the class—include the details of the case, the outcome, and what still needs to be done to ensure this does not happen to anyone else.

---

4 Available at <www.ohchr.org/en/professionalinterest/pages/crc.aspx>.

5 Available at <https://undocs.org/A/RES/61/295>.

6 Available at <www.mmiwg-ffada.ca/wp-content/uploads/2019/06/Executive_Summary.pdf>.

CONNECTIONS TO INDIGENOUS RESOURCES

Books

We Dream Medicine Dreams, by Lisa Boivin (HighWater Press, 2021; ages 6–8/grades K–2).
In this picture book, a little girl connects with the knowledge of her ancestors on how to live a good life and must lean on these teachings when her grandfather becomes sick.

Siha Tooskin Knows the Best Medicine, by Charlene Bearhead and Wilson Bearhead (HighWater Press, 2020; ages 9–11/grades 3–5).
In this book, an 11-year-old Nakota boy and his Mugoshin (grandmother) reflect on the healing properties of plants and how they have been used to treat the mind and body since before there were clinics and hospitals.

Online

Their Voices Will Guide Us: Student and Youth Engagement Guide, by Charlene Bearhead (National Inquiry into Missing and Murdered Indigenous Women and Girls, 2019). <www.mmiwg-ffada.ca/wp-content/uploads/2018/11/NIMMIWG-THEIR-VOICES-WILL-GUIDE-US.pdf>.
This resource guides educators in initiating discussions around violence against women, including root causes, and provides extensive resources, book suggestions for K–12, and activities to highlight Indigenous resilience.

Gallery of Artistic Expressions, National Inquiry into Missing and Murdered Indigenous Women and Girls. <www.mmiwg-ffada.ca/artists-list>.
This project highlights hundreds of artistic expressions gifted to the National Inquiry through the Truth Gathering Process. The collection of artworks and creative expressions could support learning around the Connected Concepts for Lisa Boivin's work in multimodal ways.

PART THREE

RESTORING

P ART 3: RESTORING explores the idea of stories translating *to* and *through* writing and representation in contemporary culture and media, intergenerational stories, physical environments and places, and digital spaces. Part of restoring is thinking about what is possible.

Charlene and Wilson Bearhead refer to the holistic process of engaging through listening and sharing. It is important that stories and storytellers are respected and given the necessary space to be heard and the time to resonate with an audience. In discussion of the storywork principle of **reverence**, Stó:lō scholar Dr. Jo-ann Archibald Q'um Q'um Xiiem reminds readers/listeners to maintain reverence for these stories and ask how we can prepare "to create a story environment that lets the spiritual nature of the story breathe."[1] When engaging with story or inviting storytellers or Knowledge Keepers to share in your classroom, it is important to respect appropriate protocols before, during, and after.

When Sonya Ballantyne questions why she is not on *Star Trek* and Elizabeth LaPensée questions the lack of Indigenous representation in video games, they are revealing the absence of representation or the misrepresentation of their ancestry in the stories they are hearing and seeing. Restoring Indigenous voices is a key aspect of the curriculum of resurgence and educators can take this on as a way of taking **responsibility** every day. We propose some ways you and your students can act to correct this imbalance

---

1   Jo-ann Archibald Q'um Q'um Xiiem, "Finding the Bone Needle Through Indigenous Story-work," in *Indigenous Knowledge Systems and Research Methodologies: Local Solutions and Global Opportunities*, eds. Elizabeth Sumida Huaman and Nathan D. Martin (Toronto: Canadian Scholars, 2020), 25. In each part overview, we focus on four of Indigenous scholar Dr. Jo-ann Archibald Q'um Q'um Xiiem's (Stó:lō and St'át'imc) storywork principles for becoming story-ready: respect, responsibility, reverence, and reciprocity. See Part Overviews: Becoming Story-Ready on page 7 for a description of these principles.

in the Educator Inquiry and Actions, Talking Back, and Inquiry sections for each text.

Reanna Merasty moves us into thinking about the underlying designs of built environments as a site for disrupting existing narratives. She talks about how designs are influenced by consultation with community. This demonstrates a type of **respect** for stories, even the ones we have not yet heard.

The authors in this section share the ways they draw on the restorative aspect of stories. What contributes to the strength of a story? How do stories transcend time and place? How does your teaching practice nurture **reciprocity** through story sharing? As you learn from the texts in this section, consider how you can reinforce the reciprocal relationships that come from reading these stories and extend the flow of learning beyond the page and into your classroom and community.

"Paper, the very tool that

was used in Eurocentric attempts to

quash our age-old system, is now a

healing tool in Indigenous hands."

Stories Are Resurgence

CHARLENE BEARHEAD (she/her/hers), an educator and Indigenous education advocate living in Treaty 6 Territory (central Alberta), is director of reconciliation for *Canadian Geographic*. She was the first education lead for the National Centre for Truth and Reconciliation and the education coordinator for the National Inquiry into Missing and Murdered Indigenous Women and Girls. Charlene, with her husband, Wilson, is author of the Siha Tooskin Knows series.

WILSON BEARHEAD (he/him/his) is a Nakota Elder and Wabamun Lake First Nation member in Treaty 6 Territory (central Alberta). A recent recipient of the Canadian Teachers' Federation Indigenous Elder Award, he co-wrote the Siha Tooskin Knows series with his wife, Charlene. Wilson is a board member for the Roots of Resilience Education Foundation.

———

STORYTELLING HAS BEEN at the core of life for Indigenous people from the very beginning of time. It is the way that genealogy, ceremony, and survival have been gifted from one generation to the next since time immemorial. Unlike communication in a Western, colonial context, there is no prescription for how the stories are shared through Indigenous ways. They are an offering of wisdom, knowledge, perspectives, and teachings and are shared in a way that honours the storyteller's voice, experience, and personality. The sharing of stories is personal, a reflection of relationship between the storyteller and the story receiver. Each individual has a role in interpreting the meaning and applying the message to life.

In contemporary times we have different ways to share our stories. We find ourselves looking to print and electronic dissemination of our stories, following a long period of time in which the interruption in our traditional ways was strategic and purposeful. Paper, the very tool that was used in Eurocentric attempts to quash our age-old system, is now a healing tool in Indigenous hands. Books give us the opportunity to share our stories widely because we can't sit with everyone at the same time. Books offer a unique way to reach one another, to understand one another, to learn more, and even to share our visions, enhanced by the offering of powerful illustrations. There is power in story; when we share stories, we build understanding and relationships. We connect with one another on a whole different level.

We can all relate to that feeling we get when we sit back and listen to a gifted storyteller: the energy in the storyteller's voice, the spirit behind the story that comes from their own personal connection to the tales and teachings, and the images they elicit in our minds through their sharing. Those are special moments to be sure, but not everyone is blessed with such opportunities. When we take these stories and our storytelling traditions and put them to paper, we offer ourselves to children in a way that means we are there for them at all times. We offer comfort and a sense of belonging to children, and adults, who might not have anyone in their lives or communities to be there for them in this way.

When we put our stories to paper, and especially when we enhance the reader's experience visually through powerful imagery, words, and illustrations, we support teachers, parents, grandparents, and others in offering stories and teachings to children. We gift them the opportunity to share the stories and to learn together. In turn, they become our voices, bringing their own energy and connection to the experience.

The great storytellers of the past have gone on, but the gifts of stories live on in us. By sharing our stories in print, we may just be offering a piece of a story to someone else who also has a connection to that story...perhaps one that was not finished before their teacher passed on. Taking storytelling to paper allows us to connect with one another in ways that we might not otherwise experience: we meet in the story even if not in the flesh.

We have been given a gift; we are living in a time of resurgence of spirit, culture, story, and connection. The stories that have waited within us for so long are emerging and they are finding their way onto paper and the canvas in many forms. We offer a new way of reaching back, deep within ourselves and our connection to spirit, to bring these stories to the light to be shared as they were meant to be shared. As storytellers—authors and artists—the gift that we have to offer is to preserve our stories, to inspire in the present and be carried into the future.

Educator Connections

Read the editors' thoughts and engage in reflection. Respond to the questions that follow on your own or with your colleague(s).

PERSONAL REFLECTIONS

Christine: For me, reading this piece validated the importance of this book. We wanted to bring together all types of stories from all over the land, so teachers and students can engage with this wisdom at their own pace. I am grateful to live in this time of resurgence. Charlene Bearhead and Wilson Bearhead explain, "The sharing of stories is personal, a reflection of relationship between the storyteller and the story receiver," and I am left wondering how this relationship can transcend time and space so that our stories can be told and shared widely. What does Indigenous storytelling look like in a virtual space?

Katya: When I think of the idea of stories, I can't help but feel personally connected. When I lost my dad, the value of stories made more sense to me. I wanted my children to know him although they had very little time with him. I am learning that through story I come to know and understand my dad differently. When I think of the stories I have heard Elders share, I have noticed that those stories linger and their meanings change over time. I have found it quite amazing how stories stay with you, and yet I now see how much sharing and community support is needed to keep stories alive.

- What do the authors mean when they talk about the "power in story"? Discuss how story can become a restorative tool for your class or school learning community.

- Think about what restoring stories looks like for the students and grade level you teach. How might story become more central in your practice?

- Look into the forms of stories that are accessible in your classroom and school libraries. Consider where these books are placed and how they are categorized. How can you improve this?

- Share teaching and learning stories that have stayed with you.

- Create a visual metaphor or simile for stories to describe their significance in your life.

Classroom Connections

Introduce to students the narrative and the Connected Concepts you wish to focus on. Use the following questions, prompts, and resource suggestions to guide student learning.

CONNECTED CONCEPTS

- Sharing stories

- Oral storytelling

- Telling your story

CONNECTING TO SELF: PROMPTS FOR PERSONAL REFLECTION

Beginning
- What are some of your favourite stories?
- How do you like to receive stories? By reading them? Listening to an audiobook? Having someone tell you a story?
- What is something you have learned from a story?

Bridging
- What makes a great storyteller?
- What are the elements of a story?
- What is the significance of oral storytelling in Indigenous culture?

Beyond
- Whose stories do you hear most often? Whose stories haven't you heard?
- What does "time immemorial" mean to you?
- How do stories transcend time and place?

CONNECTING TO COMMUNITY: PROMPTS FOR LEARNING CIRCLES

Beginning
- Share your favourite story.
- Discuss what makes stories memorable.

Bridging
- Share something you have learned from a story.
- Discuss how hearing only one story about a certain group of people can influence your thoughts and opinions about them.

Beyond
- Discuss what the authors mean when they talk about the "power in story."
- Share how you think this piece relates to the theme of restoring.

This type of storytelling as a form of knowledge and power in action talks back to dominant colonial systems and takes back power by simultaneously restoring and re-storying.

- **Problem exposing:** The authors state, "Paper, the very tool that was used in Eurocentric attempts to quash our age-old system, is now a healing tool in Indigenous hands." Look at stories that are overrepresented or misunderstood. What is another side of the story?[1] Practise writing or sharing a counter-story.

  Who is a storyteller that pushes the boundaries? It may help to think of storytelling in a broad way. Check out stories told by Indigenous artists in a variety of forms. The National Film Board offers many inspirations.

- **Juxtaposing:** Look at KC Adams's *Perception* photo series.[2] Reflect on where stereotypes come from and how they become dangerous. How do the sources of stereotypes differ from the real stories? Create your own "perception" image showing how you may be perceived versus reality to challenge the stereotypes that people place on you. What words would you use to quash those stereotypes?

INQUIRY

❭ **Beginning**

- What is your story? How do you tell your story? Explore the various technologies that can be used to share stories (for example, digital modes, online platforms, storyboards, YouTube).

---

1   For more on the importance of representation in literature and avoiding using one story to represent a particular group or culture, see "The Danger of a Single Story," by Nigerian novelist Chimamanda Ngozi Adichie (TEDGlobal, 2009), www.ted.com/talks/chimamanda_ngozi_adichie_the_danger_of_a_single_story/transcript?language=en.

2   Available at <www.kcadams.net/art/photography/Perception/PerceptionKim.html>.

⊳ Bridging

- How are stories shared, communicated, and preserved for generations? Select a culture and research its storytelling practices through the ages.

- How is storytelling changing due to technology? Research digital storytelling practices such as audiobooks, podcasts, and ebooks and explore how these new options are changing the storytelling landscape.

⬤ Beyond

- Listen to a podcast by an Indigenous author—for example, "The Truth About Stories: A Native Narrative" by Thomas King.[3] Why is storytelling important?

- Who has the right to tell and share cultural stories? Explore the concept of cultural appropriation as it relates to Indigenous stories; as a reference, see "The Difference Between Cultural Appreciation and Appropriation," by David A. Robertson.[4] How is this concept different from or similar to authors writing about cultures and experiences different than their own?

CONNECTIONS TO INDIGENOUS RESOURCES

Books

Meennunyakaa/Blueberry Patch, by Jennifer Leason (Theytus Books, 2019; ages 6–8/grades 1–3).

This dual-language book (written in Anishinaabemowin and English) offers an Elder's vivid memories of picking blueberries each summer, showing how Indigenous knowledge is shared through story.

---

3   CBC Massey Lectures, 2003, www.cbc.ca/radio/ideas the-2003-cbc-massey-lectures -the-truth-about-stories-a-native-narrative-1.2946870.

4   *Cottage Life*, June 30, 2021, cottagelife.com/general/the-difference-between-cultural -appreciation-and-appropriation.

The Eagle Mother, by Hetxw'ms Gyetxw Brett D. Huson (HighWater Press, 2020; ages 9–11/grades 4–6).
Huson, from the Gitxsan Nation, understands the importance of storytelling as a way of teaching and learning. *The Eagle Mother* tells the story of a family of eagles, which are sacred and symbolic to many Indigenous peoples.

Siha Tooskin Knows the Love of the Dance, by Charlene Bearhead and Wilson Bearhead (HighWater Press, 2020; ages 9–11/grades 3–5).
In this book, Siha Tooskin's friend attends his first powwow, learning about the dances performed there and their beautiful traditions.

Siha Tooskin Knows the Sacred Eagle Feather, by Charlene Bearhead and Wilson Bearhead (HighWater Press, 2020; ages 9–11/grades 3–5).
In this book, an 11-year-old Nakota boy learns the teachings of where eagle feathers come from and why they are so sacred.

In Search of April Raintree: Critical Edition, by Beatrice Mosionier (Portage & Main Press, 1999).
This edition of the powerful and moving story of two Métis sisters who grow up in the child welfare system includes 10 critical essays, which present ideas for debate and attest to the continuing power of Mosionier's story.

Online
"The Truth About Stories: A Native Narrative," by Thomas King (CBC Massey Lectures, 2003). <www.cbc.ca/radio/ideas/the-2003-cbc-massey -lectures-the-truth-about-stories-a-native-narrative-1.2946870>.
In this series, the award-winning author and scholar looks at Indigenous culture's deep relationship to storytelling, discussing stories told by and about Indigenous people.

Red Rising Magazine. <www.redrising.ca>.
An annual collection of stories, poetry, essays, and artwork by Indigenous authors, youth, and community members.

Why Am I Not on *Star Trek?*

SONYA BALLANTYNE is a Swampy Cree writer, filmmaker, and speaker originally from Misipawistik Cree Nation. As founder and creative director of Code Breaker Films, she is the creator of award-winning films such as *Crash Site* (2015) and *Eagle Girl* (2019). Her published works include the children's book *Kerri Berry Lynn,* as well as contributions to anthologies such as *Pros and Comic Cons* and *Women Love Wrestling*. She has also written for television, including APTN's *Taken,* TVO's *Wolf-Joe,* and the forthcoming *Builder Brothers' Dream Factory*.

WHEN I FIRST found out that writers get paid to write books, I knew, even at four years old, that writing was my sort of scam. My dad asked me what I wanted to be when I grew up and I said, "Daddy! I want to be a marine biologist, a writer, or a pro wrestler!" Since all three careers seemed equally likely for a Cree girl growing up on a Rez, my dad wished me luck.

As a professional writer, I've often felt pressure to tell "authentic" Native stories. I never knew exactly what was meant by that.

The only time I ever saw Native people on TV was when my mum would watch *North of 60*. I would hear the theme song of that show right after watching something like *The Simpsons*, and I would immediately pass out from boredom. When people asked why I didn't like the show, I would say, "They live on a reserve! If I wanted to see that, I'd go sit on the porch."

Yes, my favourite shows were things like *The Simpsons, The Fresh Prince of Bel-Air*, and *Star Trek: The Next Generation* (ST: TNG). I adored ST: TNG. I faced a lot of racism growing up and was often made to feel that being a Cree girl put me at a disadvantage in the world.

"I write about women and girls who exist in the present and the future."

Watching *ST: TNG*, I saw a world where my being a Cree girl would not matter. And I saw the possibility there would be a place for me in that future.

However, even my beloved *TNG* could annoy me. There was an episode where Captain Picard and the *Enterprise* were helping relocate a bunch of Native Americans that had settled on a planet that was being given to an alien race by the Federation. Even at five years old, I was so annoyed that people like me were still getting kicked out of places two hundred years in the future.

People like me were only seen in movies and on TV if something negative happened, or if we were being portrayed like we were long dead. My hometown of Misipawistik, Manitoba, was only ever shown on the news when a crime had been committed or a tragedy had occurred. A Native woman would only ever be mentioned in the news for the same reason.

Since I could hold a crayon, I've been writing, though when I was a teenager, I stopped. The back of the books in my English class all showed white guys who had university education. At the time, I thought I would have to write the way they did to be successful. I couldn't find myself in those books and didn't write anything for almost five years. It didn't feel "right." The world doesn't need me to write like Clive Barker because there's already a Clive Barker. I need to write like Sonya.

The important thing for storytellers, especially Indigenous ones, is to tell stories their own way. When I began writing again in my own way, I got noticed for it. I wrote the stories I wanted with heroes that looked like me or my mother. They'd be about sisters dealing with grief with the help of a superheroine (my film *Crash Site*), a little girl who wants to be powerful enough to save her grandma (*Eagle Girl*), or a woman trying to understand her mysterious grandmother (*Nosisim*).

I write about women and girls who exist in the present and the future. I've grown bored with the stories that show women like me stuck in the past or not even present. It is my goal to change the narrative, and as a writer, I feel that I am in a position to do that.

We are capable of changing the world even in small ways. When I used to see my home community on CBC, it was never for a positive reason. Now, sometimes when Misipawistik is mentioned on the news, it's because Mattel has named me a Barbie Role Model or something like that:

But the more Ballantyne reflected on being named a Barbie Role Model, the more she realized it was an opportunity. Growing up in Misipawistik Cree Nation in northern Manitoba, she didn't see herself on TV, or in movies, or in her little sister's blond-haired Barbie dolls. Challenging stereotypes and providing positive, empowering representations of Indigenous people has been a major through-line in her work as a filmmaker and, now, as an author.[1]

As a child, I saw a gap in the types of stories being told to me. I was always a storyteller, and when I saw that this gap wasn't being filled, I felt it was my duty to try and fill it. This wasn't because I thought I was the chosen one for it—I did it because I thought if I started something, others would help me finish it.

I learned a lot about myself from *Star Trek*, but I realized that no one was going to put me in that future unless I started mining the dilithium crystals to get us there. So, as a wise man once said, "Live long and prosper," and that's what I intend to do.

---

1   Jen Zoratti, "In a Barbie World: As Mattel Role Model, Cree Filmmaker/Author Empowers Indigenous People, Challenges Stereotypes," *Winnipeg Free Press*, January 18, 2019, www.winnipegfreepress.com/arts-and-life/life/in-a-barbie-world-504545652.html.

Educator Connections

Read the editors' thoughts and engage in reflection. Respond to the questions that follow on your own or with your colleague(s).

PERSONAL REFLECTIONS

Christine: Sonya Ballantyne's essay resonates with me as an Indigenous person because I had the same experiences growing up, only seeing people who look like me represented on TV during the six o'clock news because something tragic or criminal had happened. In fact, a few years ago, I read an article by Indigenous journalist Duncan McCue where he addresses this and says, "An elder once told me the only way an Indian would make it on the news is if he or she were one of the 4Ds: drumming, dancing, drunk or dead."[2] Reflecting on my school experience, I barely learned anything about Indigenous people, period. I remember reading *April Raintree* in high school and that was my first time reading a story about Indigenous people. I remember relating to the trauma the main characters experienced and crying at how pervasive trauma is in our communities. Today, I am proud to be able to help shift the narrative away from Indigenous trauma to show more about the resilience and strength in our communities. I have no doubt that we will soon see an Indigenous astronaut in both reality and literature.

Katya: Sonya Ballantyne's words provide such guidance for teachers to ensure youth see positive representations of themselves and their cultures in schools and in the many types of texts beyond school contexts. She addresses omissions and misrepresentations that reveal a hidden curriculum that teaches the superiority of white male authors'

---

2   "What It Takes for Aboriginal People to Make the News," CBC News, January 29, 2014, www.cbc.ca/news/indigenous/what-it-takes-for-aboriginal-people-to-make-the-news -1.2514466.

perspectives and static misrepresentations of Indigenous peoples and communities. Her personality makes an entrance through her works! I can see how kids would relate to them and be inspired to find their own voices. As individuals find their voices, it will change the narratives of Canada.

EDUCATOR INQUIRY AND ACTIONS

- Look at your professional resource collection. How many of these resources are written by Indigenous authors or incorporate Indigenous worldviews?

- As an educator, how can you ensure that Indigenous people and cultures are reflected positively and in contemporary ways in the classroom?

- Has your identity been reflected in texts (print, visual, online, etc.)? How has it been reflected? What effect has this had on you as a teacher?

- Include empowering representations of Indigenous peoples and role models from your local context in your educational environment. Think about the many ways you can communicate this at the school level. Posting information on the walls is a start, but be creative and get students involved.

- How can you change the quantity, quality, and range of representation in your list of go-to classroom and school resources?

Classroom Connections

Introduce to students the narrative and the Connected Concepts you wish to focus on. Use the following questions, prompts, and resource suggestions to guide student learning.

- Representation in literature/media

- Role models

- Counter-stories[3]

CONNECTING TO SELF: PROMPTS FOR PERSONAL REFLECTION

⟩ Beginning

- Who are your role models and heroes?

- Do you have any role models or heroes that look like you?

▶ Bridging

- Of the texts we've read, seen, and listened to, which did you connect to the most and why?

- If you could create a story in the medium of your choice (for example, book, film, podcast), what would it be about?

● Beyond

- Have you ever felt that you are at a disadvantage because of who you are?

- Do you see Indigenous people represented in media? Where? How?

CONNECTING TO COMMUNITY: PROMPTS FOR LEARNING CIRCLES

⟩ Beginning

- Describe your role models and heroes.

- Share a TV show that you would like to be on and explain why you would choose this show.

---

3   For more on counter-stories, see Daniel G. Solórzano and Tara J. Yosso, "Critical Race Methodology: Counter-Storytelling as an Analytical Framework for Education Research," *Qualitative Inquiry* 8, no. 1 (2002): 23–44.

▶ Bridging

- Of the texts we've read, seen, and listened to, describe one that you connected to strongly and what made you feel connected to it.

- Share how you think Sonya Ballantyne is "changing the narrative."

- Describe what you would do if you could change the world "even in small ways."

● Beyond

- Discuss the term *representation* and what it means to you.

- Discuss the term *privilege*. (Have you ever participated in a privilege walk? Share what you remember about this experience.)

TALKING BACK

Sonya Ballantyne's personal essay talks back to her experience of noticing a gap in the stories she was hearing or being told. Her work as a writer centres on talking back to misrepresentations or under-representations of her Swampy Cree identity in stories and media.

- **Problem exposing:** This piece exposes a major curricular issue. Indigenous perspectives have been part of a null curriculum (not taught in schools),[4] or a hidden curriculum that misrepresented, omitted, or misunderstood the history, worldviews, and knowledges of Indigenous peoples.[5] How can you improve representation in your school or classroom library?

---

4   For more on null curriculum, see Elliot Eisner, "The Three Curricula That All Schools Teach," in *The Educational Imagination* (2nd ed.; New York: Macmillan, 1985).

5   For more on hidden curriculum, see Michael Apple, "The Hidden Curriculum and the Nature of Conflict," in *Ideology and Curriculum* (4th ed.; New York: Routledge Falmer, 2019).

- **Juxtaposing:** Look up more about Sonya Ballantyne's story of being a Barbie Role Model. How does this juxtapose with previous Barbie stories and Barbie worlds? Why is this important?

INQUIRY

〉 Beginning

- Research books that feature characters you identify with. Create a list of book recommendations with characters from various backgrounds.

❱ Bridging

- Take an inventory of books written by Indigenous authors in the school library. What are they about? Graph the themes.

- How are Black, Indigenous, and People of Colour (BIPOC) represented in the media? Inquire into empowering representations of BIPOC people in the media.

● Beyond

- Read the Truth and Reconciliation Commission's Calls to Action on Media and Reconciliation (numbers 84, 85, and 86).[6] Track news stories over the course of a week and reflect on those that include Indigenous content or perspectives. Read the Duncan McCue article mentioned in Christine's Personal Reflection as a starting point. Respond by writing to local or national media networks and encourage others to share the results of your inquiry.

- Research how Indigenous peoples have been represented in media throughout history. Present your findings.

---

6   Available at <publications.gc.ca/collections/collection_2015/trc/IR4-8-2015-eng.pdf>.

CONNECTIONS TO INDIGENOUS RESOURCES

Books

Dakwäkãda Warriors, by Cole Pauls (Conundrum Press, 2019; ages 10–12/ grades 5–7).

This dual-language young adult graphic novel was created out of the author's desire to help revitalize the language of the Southern Tutchone, which he learned growing up in Whitehorse. It tells the story of two earth protectors trying to save the world from evil pioneers and cyborg sasquatches.

The Marrow Thieves, by Cherie Dimaline (Dancing Cat Books, 2017; ages 13 and up/grades 8 and up).

This young adult novel is set in a near-future world where Indigenous people are the only ones who are able to dream. The story provides parallels between the characters' struggles to survive and current realities.

Films

Crash Site (Code Breaker Films, 2015) and *Eagle Girl* (Code Breaker Films, 2019), written and directed by Sonya Ballantyne.

These films give additional context to the range of texts Ballantyne creates, demonstrating the importance of layered identities, perspectives, and genres.

Reel Injun, directed by Neil Diamond (National Film Board, 2009).

In this documentary, Cree filmmaker Diamond looks at portrayals of North American Indigenous peoples through a century of movies.

Indigenizing Spaces: Identity in the Built Environment

REANNA MERASTY (she/her/hers) is Ininew from Barren Lands First Nation. She completed her Master of Architecture degree at the University of Manitoba and is an architectural intern at Number TEN Architectural Group. She also works with One House Many Nations as a research assistant on First Nations housing development, where her research focuses on reciprocity, Indigenous knowledge systems, and land-based pedagogy.

I GREW UP AROUND Reindeer Lake in northern Manitoba, where my grandfather educated me in traditional Indigenous architecture. Specifically, my grandfather passed on to me traditional Indigenous knowledge related to log cabin construction. Through that experience I learned that the land is engrained in us as Indigenous peoples, as it runs through our veins and fills our spirit. Our bodies are indeed children of the land. Moreover, it is my belief that we are connected to Mother Earth and all that she has to offer us. It is by that connection that we find our identity as Indigenous peoples. Mother Earth serves to influence many aspects of our life: teachings, ceremony, medicine, languages, construction, craft, and art.

Colonialism, or control over Indigenous peoples, has of course affected us in many ways, including the destruction of land and ongoing acts of assimilation and discrimination. Despite sustaining us for thousands of years, the land has been overtaken by greed and efforts to maximize economic return. The result is the destruction of habitat, ecosystems, and the living beings within. Robin Wall Kimmerer eloquently speaks to the effect

"I learned that the land is engrained in us as Indigenous peoples, as it runs through our veins and fills our spirit."

of colonialism: "In the settler mind, land was property, real estate, capital, or natural resources. But to our people, it was everything: identity, the connection to our ancestors, the home of our nonhuman kinfolk, our pharmacy, our library, the source of all that sustains us."[1]

INDIGENOUS DESIGN

The field of architecture is representative of colonial structures that have spread across Indigenous lands. However, there is an emerging effort for more representation in the field of architecture, as championed by at least 20 Indigenous architects in Canada.

For Indigenous architects, the act of regaining spaces is the purpose—spaces that move beyond mere notions of Indigenous symbolism to a deeper understanding of Indigenous culture and its application to architecture.[2] Indigenous worldviews indeed contribute understandings of space and place that are integral to human relationships with the Earth, and to Indigenous values embodied in cultural practice.

I'm convinced that the Earth influences Indigenous architectural practices, processes, and methods in reciprocity. Reciprocity mandates us to consider all who live in creation, including our nonhuman kin. This concept is used for understanding Indigenous culture and traditional beliefs because it highlights the importance of community.[3] The approaches we take to community design are evident in our relationships, specifically consultation processes designed to go beyond dialogue and timeline, into embracing long-term connections with the Indigenous community that Indigenous architects work with. The drive for Indigenous architects is to establish respectful relationships, as well as to design for and with communities.

---

1   Robin Wall Kimmerer, *Braiding Sweetgrass: Indigenous Wisdom, Scientific Knowledge and the Teachings of Plants* (Minneapolis: Milkweed Editions, 2013), 17.

2   Chris Cornelius, "Chris Cornelius: Atmosphere 2020; Next School," YouTube, March 19, 2020, www.youtube.com/watch?v=qw1TMLd0ptc, 31:30.

3   Kathleen O'Reilly-Scanlon, Christine Crowe, and Angelina Weenie, "Pathways to Understanding: 'Wahkohtowin' as a Research Methodology," *McGill Journal of Education* 39, no. 1 (Winter 2004): 29–44.

Organic versus rigid: Destruction of Indigenous lands and bodies,
by Reanna Merasty.

(Image courtesy of Reanna Merasty.)

Architectural depiction of gathering space from Indigenous Transition Education Centre project.

(Image courtesy of Reanna Merasty.)

Indigenous spaces require representation of medicine, lands, traditions, language, and structures of the local Indigenous nation. They should acknowledge the complex knowledge systems and values that vary from nation to nation, with each having their own traditions and practices. If we look to the west, for example, we see the significance of the many salmon that nourish the forest. If we look to the east, to the Great Lakes, we see the care for wild rice that sustains the Anishinaabe. If we look to the north, we see caribou herds that sustain the Dene and Inuit.

These practices of course are unique and intrinsic to place-based conditions and should be celebrated through Indigenous architecture. This new wave of designing incorporates the local land through meaningful consultation with the local Indigenous nation. For me, and I hope for more Indigenous youth pursuing careers in architecture, it is important to see Indigenous peoples in the spaces we inhabit because it is a reflection of our ancestors, and the land that sustained us for thousands of years.

Indigenous architects have been pushing the boundaries of the profession of architecture and creating space for our identities, making room for the next generation to disrupt colonial narratives and participate in creating our built environment.

Architectural depiction of residence entrance from Pritchard's Creek Healing Centre project.

(Image courtesy of Reanna Merasty.)

Architectural depiction of nibi (water) lookout from Pritchard's Creek Healing Centre project.

(Image courtesy of Reanna Merasty.)

Educator Connections

Read the editors' thoughts and engage in reflection. Respond to the questions that follow on your own or with your colleague(s).

PERSONAL REFLECTIONS

Christine: I'm a big fan of Reanna Merasty's work and I appreciate the thought that goes into her architectural creations. She talks about the teaching of reciprocity as it relates to community design. Too often we think about how the land can benefit us and not about how we can give back to the land and all of its inhabitants. Of course, as a teacher, Merasty's statement, "Indigenous spaces require representation of medicine, lands, traditions, language, and structures of the local Indigenous nation" inspires me to think about how schools and other learning spaces can be designed in this way. I am forced to ask myself how my own classroom can better represent Indigenous medicine, lands, traditions, and language.

Katya: I'm increasingly intrigued by how central place is becoming in educational discussions. Places have become disrupted as so many people have been displaced. It is interesting how Mother Earth is beginning to respond—it is as if she is calling for restorative connections. I've always been intrigued by how spaces can be designed to invite and include. Reanna Merasty's perspectives on architecture and establishing relationships and designing structures for and with communities relate to work that needs to be done among educators as well. This means developing partnerships with parents and communities—going beyond just a meet-the-teacher night or sending letters home—by designing spaces and educational opportunities that invite them into physical spaces and into meaningful dialogue about supporting the learning journey of their children. Wahkohtowin—in true partnership.

EDUCATOR INQUIRY AND ACTIONS

- Whose traditional territory is your classroom and images on? What languages have been spoken in this territory for millennia? How do you honour Indigenous nations in your practice?

- How can you commit to learning more about Indigenous nations? How can your learning environment be reimagined to better reflect Indigenous culture?

- Historically, schools as institutions have not been designed to support Indigenous ways of knowing and being. How can your school's built environment be improved? Does your school currently reflect Indigeneity and connections to land?

- As a school team, walk through the school and around the school grounds and notice what is there and what is missing. Whose story is told in the built environment?

- Find a place in your school or community that you consider an Indigenous space and reflect on what characteristics make it an Indigenous space. What materials were used to create this space? What ideas are central? What feelings are created?

- Consider the framework of designing for and with communities. As an educator, how do you design spaces that establish respectful relationships? How do you design for and with your learning community? Seek input from parents and community members when adapting existing or adding new spaces within the school (for example, what types of spaces or affordances could make the built environment more inclusive?).

- Discuss Robin Wall Kimmerer's assertion that "In the settler mind, land was property, real estate, capital, or natural resources. But to our people, it was everything: identity, the connection to our ancestors, the home of our nonhuman kinfolk, our pharmacy, our library, the source of all that sustains us." Consider an inquiry into the term *settler colonialism*.

Classroom Connections

Introduce to students the narrative and images and the Connected Concepts you wish to focus on. Use the following questions, prompts, and resource suggestions to guide student learning.

CONNECTED CONCEPTS

- Traditional and modern Indigenous architecture

- Indigenous land acknowledgments

- Places and spaces

CONNECTING TO SELF: PROMPTS FOR PERSONAL REFLECTION

Beginning

- What is your favourite room in your home? What are the characteristics of that room?

- What is a place that you love? What makes it special?

Bridging

- Which built environments do you feel connected to or most comfortable within and why?

- Whose traditional territory are you on? What nations occupied this territory historically and presently? What do you know about these nations?

Beyond

- Why is it important to see yourself in spaces and places?

- Do you feel that the land is "engrained" in you? How?

- Do you have a reciprocal relationship with the land? How might you foster this?

CONNECTING TO COMMUNITY: PROMPTS FOR LEARNING CIRCLES

> **Beginning**

* Share a fact you know about the history of the place where you live.

* Share something you know about the Indigenous nations of this land.

> **Bridging**

* Share what you know about Indigenous history or culture and where or how you learned this.

* Share something that you have been taught by Mother Earth.

* Discuss how Mother Earth affects your life.

Beyond

* Discuss the meaning of culture.

* Share your understanding of the term *worldview* and describe an example of a worldview.

* Describe how you demonstrate reciprocity with other humans and "non-human kin."

TALKING BACK

Reanna Merasty talks back to the way colonialism and built environments have transformed natural and constructed landscapes across what is now known as Canada.

* **Problem exposing:** Find an example of a place in your school (such as the office, main entrance, or parent room) that does not currently reflect Indigeneity. Analyze this space: How inclusive is it? Is it accessible? Does it feel safe? Design a more inclusive version of this space.

* **Juxtaposing:** Find a place in your school or community that you would consider an Indigenous space. Consider all the elements that you think make it an Indigenous space. What nations do you see represented?

Consider Robin Wall Kimmerer's statement: "In the settler mind, land was property, real estate, capital, or natural resources. But to our people, it was everything: identity, the connection to our ancestors, the home of our nonhuman kinfolk, our pharmacy, our library, the source of all that sustains us."[4] Find one image to represent each worldview and discuss this from both a historical and contemporary perspective.

INQUIRY

❯ Beginning

- What is the culture of the Indigenous nations whose territory you live on? Learn from a local Indigenous Elder or Knowledge Keeper and reflect on your findings.

- What are some traditional dwellings Indigenous peoples built? Look at dwellings from a variety of geographical areas or nations.

❯ Bridging

- How does geography influence buildings? Research the role of geography in architecture and write an essay to explain your findings.

- Take a walk through an urban landscape and look for evidence of Indigenous spaces or designs that signify a reclamation of space. What do you notice? What are the features of Indigenous spaces? Create a photo essay to capture your findings.

- Take a walk in a rural location or natural environment. Design a dwelling in your sketchbook that is inspired by a natural element (e.g., landform, material, or feature) that stood out during your walk.

● Beyond

- How does colonialism influence people's connections to (or disconnections from) land? Research an example of forced relocation and write an essay to describe your findings.

- How are Indigenous architects reclaiming spaces and places in Canada? Research examples of Indigenous peoples reclaiming spaces and present your findings to the class, using both pictures and words.

---

4   Kimmerer, *Braiding Sweetgrass*, 17.

CONNECTIONS TO INDIGENOUS RESOURCES

Books

The Eagle Feather, by Kevin Locke (Medicine Wheel Education, 2019; ages 4–6/grades K–1).
This meaningful story explores the themes of Indigenous ways of knowing and being, focusing on the eagle's powerful teachings.

Sus Yoo/The Bear's Medicine, by Clayton Gauthier (Theytus Books, 2019; ages 6–8/grades 1–3).
This dual-language English and Dakelh picture book uses a bear family to demonstrate the importance of relationships with the environment and how these relationships require reciprocity.

Kamik Takes the Lead, by Darryl Baker (Inhabit Media, 2020; ages 6–8/ grades 1–3).
In this book for young readers, a boy learns traditional knowledge from his uncle as he trains his sled dog. The story demonstrates the importance of patience, responsibility, and respect for animals.

Indigenous Communities in Canada series (Scholastic Canada; ages 7–9/ grades 2–4).
Each book in this series for young readers focuses on a different Indigenous community or nation (for example, Métis, Iroquois, and Cree), exploring its history, language, and cultural practices, both in the past and present.

Online

"Just What Is Indigenous Architecture?" by Tim Querengesser, *Azure Magazine*, June 8, 2018. <www.azuremagazine.com/article/indigenous -architecture-unceded/>.
This article describes *Unceded*, Canada's contribution to the 2018 Venice Architecture Biennale, which was co-curated by 17 Indigenous architects. *Unceded* was organized into rooms that corresponded to the themes of Indigeneity, resilience, sovereignty, and colonialization.

"We as Indigenous game developers

have made space for ourselves."

Games as Resurgence

ELIZABETH LAPENSÉE (she/her or they/them), PhD, is an award-winning designer, writer, artist, and researcher who creates and studies Indigenous-led media, including video games. She is Anishinaabe with family from Bay Mills, Métis, and Irish. She is an assistant professor of media and information, and writing, rhetoric, and American cultures at Michigan State University and a 2018 Guggenheim Fellow.

I'M AN '80S kid. Technology classes for me meant going to a makeshift trailer turned computer lab. My way of rebelling was to sneak in playing games during keyboarding class. One of the only games available was *The Oregon Trail*, and aside from laughing when characters with funny names "died of dysentery," I was mostly bothered by what the gameplay was saying. If Indigenous people weren't fulfilling the stereotype of circling wagons, they were there either to trade with or guide settlers. And that was it. In *The Oregon Trail* and many games since then, Indigenous characters are portrayed in relation to settlers. They are rarely given the opportunity to speak, let alone exist sovereign.

In response, this Anishinaabe, Métis, and Irish geek set out to work. I started off with projects like modding (meaning modifying) *Super Mario Bros.* (by adding a thunderbird power-up, obviously) and running a text-based role-playing community. Since then, I've bounced between the roles of designer, artist, and writer while developing games. I filled all those roles in the lightning-searing side-scroller *Thunderbird Strike*. We as Indigenous game developers have made space for ourselves through games such as *Ehdrigohr, Never Alone, Spirits of Spring, Guardian Maia, Neofeud, Treachery in Beatdown City, Terra Nova, Don't Wake the Night, Hold My Hand, Umurangi Generation, Button City*, and *Hill Agency*, with so many more on the way.

For me, a standout experience was working on *When Rivers Were Trails*,[1] an Indigenous spin on a 2D point-and-click adventure game in which *The Oregon Trail* meets *Where the Water Tastes Like Wine*. The comic aesthetic is thanks to the brilliant Weshoyot Alvitre. The merging of traditional and contemporary music stems from Apsáalooke rapper and fancy dancer Supaman. Incredibly, there are over a hundred character scenarios written by 30 Indigenous writers. The ability to involve so many Indigenous contributors was thanks to the game being funded by the San Manuel Band of Mission Indians through the Indian Land Tenure Foundation. It thus speaks to what is possible when the development process is truly sovereign.

When Rivers Were Trails came about because the Indian Land Tenure Foundation saw the need to actively respond to concerns regarding the lack of Indigenous-led land-centred knowledge in schools. As a result, they collaborated with Indigenous educators and Knowledge Carriers on the Lessons of Our Land curriculum. The curriculum was well received, but they wanted to push further by working toward an interactive way of engaging in knowledge. Co-creative director Nichlas Emmons was informed of my work and took a chance on me as an Indigenous designer without a company. We collaborated with the Games for Entertainment and Learning Lab at Michigan State University through an Indigenous-led development process that included self-determined representations with the aim of Indigenizing education.

Since then, my childhood daydream of having an Indigenous-led game in schools to make up for the issues of *The Oregon Trail* has come true. The next generations will experience better. They'll know the truth of the impact of colonization and the falsehoods of westward expansion. *When Rivers Were Trails* was designed specifically for middle-school and high-school classrooms and focuses on Indigenous perspectives on history, expressing cultures, encouraging land recovery, and conveying land-management practices.

---

[1] *When Rivers Were Trails* can be downloaded from the Indian Land Tenure Foundation's website: <indianlandtenure.itch.io/when-rivers-were-trails>.

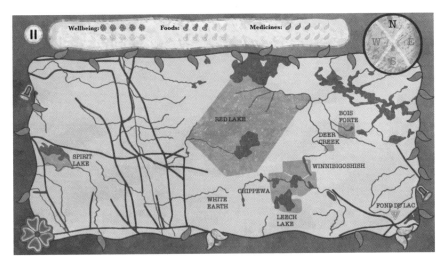

Map from *When Rivers Were Trails*.
(Image courtesy of Indian Land Tenure Foundation, 2019.)

Screenshot from *When Rivers Were Trails*.
(Image courtesy of Indian Land Tenure Foundation, 2019.)

Screenshot from *When Rivers Were Trails*.
(Image courtesy of Indian Land Tenure Foundation, 2019.)

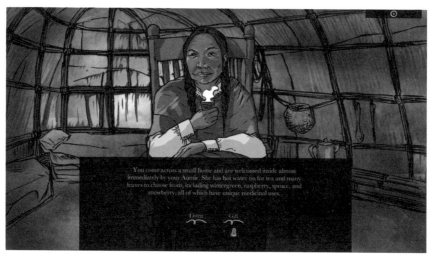

Screenshot from *When Rivers Were Trails*.
(Image courtesy of Indian Land Tenure Foundation, 2019.)

As a player, you take on the role of an Anishinaabe person who is displaced in Minnesota—due to the impact of allotment acts on Indigenous communities—and, as a result, head to California in the 1890s. You travel through Minnesota, the Dakotas, Montana, Idaho, Washington, Oregon, and California, interacting along the way with people from nations including Dakota, Lakota, Blackfeet, Apsáalooke, Nimiipuu, and many more, each with their own cultural representation, thanks to the many writers involved.

The journey changes from game to game as you encounter land, waters, minerals, stars, animals, plants, Indigenous people, and adversaries such as Indian agents. You are challenged to balance your physical, emotional, mental, and spiritual well-being with foods and medicines while making choices about contributing to resistances, as well as trading, fishing, hunting, gifting, and honouring the life you meet.

In fact, a unique aspect of the design is in gaining and losing honour in a hidden system. I chose to hide the honour rating because it's important to play not toward what you think the game's goal is, but based on your own reactions. Your level of honour determines which version of the game story is revealed to you as you transition from map to map during the journey. Are you hearing the version that emphasizes resistance? Or the one that falls back on the government's spin of colonization?

It's up to each player to determine how they react during their journey, making both the game development process and the player's experience one of enacting sovereignty. *When Rivers Were Trails* proves that it's possible to have an award-winning Indigenous-led game that blurs the boundaries between education and entertainment. And there are so many games yet to come that will further expand the possibilities for Indigenous resurgence through gameplay.

·

Educator Connections

Read the editors' thoughts and engage in reflection. Respond to the questions that follow on your own or with your colleague(s).

PERSONAL REFLECTIONS

Christine: I absolutely love Elizabeth LaPensée's video game idea! I admire her work ethic and determination—she saw a lack of Indigenous representation in video games and "set out to work." In this personal essay, she discusses how the Indian Land Tenure Foundation noticed a "lack of Indigenous-led land-centred knowledge in schools," which prompted them to collaborate with the community and create a whole new curriculum along with the game LaPensée developed! I find myself daydreaming about the exciting possibilities technology and video games can produce within the field of Indigenous education. I am also reflecting on my own teaching practice and how there is a lack of Indigenous-led land-centred knowledge in my school. How might technology be a solution to this?

Katya: I am out of my element when it comes to gaming! I do, however, see its incredible potential power to restore representations in refreshing ways and expand understandings and engagement with curriculum. I am fascinated with the way contemporary and traditional aspects are melded together in *When Rivers Were Trails*, and the hidden honour system within makes me want to try this out. What an interesting way of teaching and living and learning through the challenges of balancing holistic aspects of well-being, making healthy choices, and enacting sovereignty. I can see so many young people being inspired by this blurring of entertainment and education in such an innovative way.

- How is technology supporting Indigenous resurgence and restoring Indigenous identities?

- Do you notice a lack of Indigenous-led land-centred knowledge in your school? How can you work to address this?

- Find an Indigenous-designed game that supports land-based learning. (See the link to Elizabeth LaPensée's website in the Connections to Indigenous Resources section for some initiating resources.)

- What are allotment acts and what has been their impact on Indigenous peoples?

- How do you use technology in your practice?

- What do you know about gaming? Look up some of the Indigenous games listed in LaPensée's essay that are available online and make time to play. You can also take a walk-through of a game on YouTube. (Note: Walk-through videos and trailers are available for games such as *Never Alone*, which represents stories and traditions of Iñupiat people.) Then, discuss with colleagues the video game you played or watched. What was the story? What journey did you take? What did you learn or experience? How did you feel?

- If you aren't currently playing video games for educational purposes, are there other ways you might transform play-based activities in your classroom? How can you gamify your existing practices? Or reflect on how classrooms and school life are already gamified.

- Discuss something new or surprising you learned from Elizabeth LaPensée's essay.

- Design a professional learning day for your school team that incorporates the idea of *"tradigital* knowledge," which refers to the "harmony of traditional knowledge and its digital expressions, rather than their alleged contradiction."[2]

- Using an existing game, discuss how you could design a space for yourself within the gamified environment.

- As you are reading this collection of cultural expressions or preparing to teach a particular concept in science or social studies, look for Indigenous video games that connect to the topic you're studying. You can use these to enhance the way students of all ages engage with the issues.

- Discuss the meaning and significance of Elizabeth LaPensée's statement, "It thus speaks to what is possible when the development process is truly sovereign." To support this work, look up more Indigenous video-game designers to hear their stories.

---

2   See Gabrielle Hughes, "*Tradigital* Knowledge? Indigenous Video Games, Copyright, and the Protection of Traditional Knowledge," in *The Interactive Past: Archaeology, Heritage, and Video Games*, eds. Angus A. A. Mol et al. (Leiden, Netherlands: Sidestone Press, 2017), 34.

Classroom Connections

Introduce to students the narrative and images and the Connected Concepts you wish to focus on. Use the following questions, prompts, and resource suggestions to guide student learning.

CONNECTED CONCEPTS

- Land-based education

- Indigenous games

- Technology

CONNECTING TO SELF: PROMPTS FOR PERSONAL REFLECTION

Beginning

- Do you see people who look like you in the media?

- What is your favourite thing to do on the land?

- Have you ever played an Indigenous-designed video game?

Bridging

- What can we learn from the land?

- How do games help you learn?

- What makes the images from *When Rivers Were Trails* stand out to you?

Beyond

- What values do games teach us?

- Do you feel like people from your culture are accurately represented in the media? Why or why not?

- Why do you think video games are so popular?

CONNECTING TO COMMUNITY: PROMPTS FOR LEARNING CIRCLES

❯ Beginning

- Share your favourite game and explain why you like it.

- Share something you've learned from a game.

❯ Bridging

- Share your favourite video-game character and an experience they encountered.

- Discuss what you think are the positives and negatives of gaming.

● Beyond

- Discuss something new or surprising that you learned from Elizabeth LaPensée's essay.

- Share your thoughts and ideas about video games in schools.

TALKING BACK

This essay discusses the power of video-game writers and how the perspectives of the writers who worked on *When Rivers Were Trails* helped to reflect many Indigenous nations. This actively talks back to a singular "pan-Indigenous" identity, which is problematic because it minimizes diversity among nations. How might you talk back to pan-Indigenous approaches by giving specificity or seeking deeper understanding?

- **Problem exposing:** Look at a video game you play and find a way to rewrite some of the rules or introduce another character you identify with. What would be their special skill or attribute? Design your own power-ups. Or explore digital platforms such as *Minecraft* to create a community to design a space collaboratively.

- **Juxtaposing:** Compare and contrast the images from *When Rivers Were Trails* with screenshots from another popular video game. Are cultural elements visible? How are they displayed? Whose culture is most visible?

) **Beginning**

- What values are important to the Indigenous nation whose territory you are on? Learn from a local Elder or Knowledge Keeper and record your findings. How might these values be incorporated into a game?

- Look up Indigenous-designed video games. Watch a walk-through or gameplay and write your own trailer to share an overview of the game.

- How are traditional knowledges being translated into digital spaces?

) **Bridging**

- How can we take care of the land? Create a video of you demonstrating how young people can take care of the land.

- Play an Indigenous-designed video game. What story does it tell? What challenges did you encounter? What actions did you take and what were the effects of your choices? What did you learn?

- Design a plan for how video games should be used in schools. Consider who would use the games and for what purpose, and where and when they would play and for how long. Present a rationale for your ideas. Propose this plan to your class.

● **Beyond**

- How are Indigenous people represented in the media? How are other groups of people represented in the media? What groups are not represented in the media at all? Compare and contrast media representation of various groups throughout the years.

- What do you think "*tradigital* knowledge" is and could be?

- Work in groups on a "game jam" (design a video game collaboratively). Consider the following: What story do you want to tell? What might be the challenges? What actions would the characters take? For example, you could begin with an inquiry such as: What are some sustainable land management practices that Indigenous nations have been using for centuries? Record your findings in a series of digital images like the screenshots included with this essay.

CONNECTIONS TO INDIGENOUS RESOURCES

Online

Elizabeth LaPensée: Games. <www.elizabethlapensee.com/#/games>.
LaPensée's website provides more information about her creative works,
including her video games, comics, artwork, animation, publications, and
resources in Anishinaabemowin.

Honour Water. <www.honourwater.com/about#bio>.
Honour Water, another example of Elizabeth LaPensée's work, is a singing
game that passes on songs and water teachings in Anishinaabemowin.

iNdigital Space, imagineNATIVE. <indigital.imaginenative.org/home.html>.
ImagineNATIVE is an organization that hosts an Indigenous film and media
arts festival and promotes Indigenous screen content through its iNdigital initiative. This site showcases digital creations and exhibitions by many
Indigenous artists, and offers extensive resources, workshops, and events.

"Indigenous Games You Should Download," *Muskrat Magazine*, April 1,
2016..
This article describes six video games that offer Indigenous-inspired adventures, including two Elizabeth LaPensée projects.

"First Nations Gamer Calls Out Popular Video Game's 'Pro-Genocide' Talk
Reminding Him of Residential Schools," by Logan Turner, CBC News, July
16, 2021. <www.cbc.ca/news/canada/thunder-bay/video-game-insensitive
-dialogue-1.6104700>.
This article discusses Indigenous representation in video games and would
be a great reference when discussing issues around digital games as acts of
sovereignty.

PART FOUR

RECONNECTING

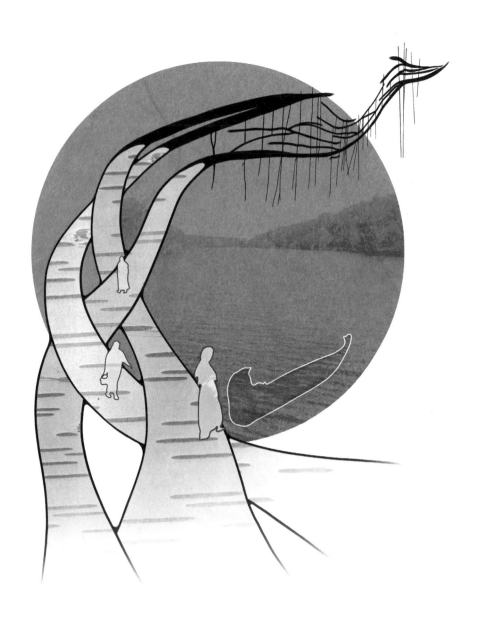

THE TEXTS FEATURED in part 4 centre around the theme of reconnecting with culture and identity. This section offers reminders of how to reconnect ideas, practices, and works to bridge personal experiences and professional practices. The texts challenge us to make meaning metaphorically and symbolically, and in ways that approach time as fluid and cyclical rather than linear. You may need to engage with each text several times to read between the lines, and then listen between the lines. We encourage you to listen and view deeply for disconnections and (re)connections before bringing the texts and their topics into your classroom.

Preparing to learn from these texts means being open to and **respectful** of the many ways we make meaning.[1] Honour the depth of meaning that comes from multimodal texts and thinking through metaphors. Nicola Campbell's poems are uniquely formatted and may challenge you as a reader. To help students engage with these poems, try to uncover how Campbell might have begun writing and thinking through the design process. Take time to explore the aesthetics of the text (for example, font size, use of lowercase and uppercase letters) and the shape of the poems with your students.

Engaging with Russell Wallace's piece requires a **reverence** for tradition. His writing about how traditions change over time and have been impacted by colonialism can be used as a starting point for discussions about culture, spirituality, and religious beliefs in your classroom. How can you create a safe

---

1   In each part overview, we focus on four of Indigenous scholar Dr. Jo-ann Archibald Q'um Q'um Xiiem's (Stó:lō and St'át'imc) storywork principles for becoming story-ready: respect, responsibility, reverence, and reciprocity. See Part Overviews: Becoming Story-Ready on page 7 for a description of these principles.

172

space for students to share in such discussions? It is important to highlight similarities and to acknowledge tensions or differences in respectful ways.

In this section, you will also read Victoria, or Biktoryias, McIntosh's words. She is a residential school Survivor. Prepare to read her words through the lens of **responsibility** as an educator. When engaging with McIntosh's work, we chose not to focus directly on the topic of residential schools, but rather on sources of strength that are evident in her works. Consider how you can balance teaching students about both trauma and resilience.

Christina Lavalley Ruddy's personal essay does not discuss residential school, but does describe feelings of being traumatized by school experiences and low self-efficacy in math as a result. She reminds us of the importance of finding ways to incorporate cultural identities into subjects such as math, which have often been approached as neutral and universal. Ruddy describes the power of doing what you love, and how sharing one's gifts with the world nourishes the body, mind, and spirit.

The knowledge shared in the texts in this section may inspire creative responses, such as concrete poetry, visual art, and metaphorical thinking, from both you and your students. As you take this learning into your work in the classroom, keep coming back to the words, works, and ideas of the voices featured here. Keep the notion of **reciprocity** central as you engage with Nicola Campbell's poems, Russell Wallace's essay, Victoria McIntosh's artwork and writing, and Christina Lavalley Ruddy's essay and images. Reference and honour their names and nations as you share with your students work that is inspired by them; how you choose to respond represents a living extension of their stories.

"we see the sacred in everything

and the sacred sees us."

"alpine mountains"
and "frog whisperers"

NICOLA I. CAMPBELL is the author of several children's books including *Shi-shi-etko, Shin-chi's Canoe* (winner of the TD Canadian Children's Literature Award), and *Stand Like a Cedar*, as well as the memoir *Spílax̱m: A Weaving of Recovery, Resilience, and Resurgence*. Nłeʔkepmx, Syilx, and Métis, from British Columbia, her stories weave cultural and land-based teachings that focus on respect, endurance, healing, and reciprocity.

I'M WRITING TO remember. I'm writing to reconnect the strands that should not have been broken. I'm writing to learn how to listen with my heart as well as to share our stories and our history in a good way, so we never forget who we are. This is one strand creating a narrative of strength, intertwining hearts, minds, and spirits, reminding ourselves of all that is good and strong. I'm writing to listen and remember the story echoes that are the voices of our ancestors as they sing back to us when we sing to the mountains, when we sing to the water, when we sing to the land. I'm writing to understand and reflect on Indigenous stories, so that our truths and our identity as Indigenous people can never again be wiped away by the colonizer.[1]

---

1   Paragraph and poems excerpted from Nicola I. Campbell, *Spílax̱m: A Weaving of Recovery, Resilience, and Resurgence* (Winnipeg: HighWater Press, 2021), 36, 37, 280.

alpine mountains

"you
    girls
        have
           ċəlċále
              all
                 over
                    your
                       faces,"
                    my
                auntie
                laughs.
surprised, we look at one another.
dark purple ċəlċále paints our cheeks, lips, and hands.
"cuzzin is purpler!" i say pointing at her. "No you are!" she points
back at me. Suzie is laughing at us but she hasn't seen herself. "let's
have a competition!" "we each have to eat fifty ċəlċále at once then see who's
purplest!" pebbles and rocks fly as we scramble up the mountainside back
to our ċəlċále patch. lightning fast we gather fifty of the fattest berries. "ready!"
Suzie and i holler. "me too!" cuzzin cups her berries to her mouth. Suzie & i copy
her. all of a sudden she screams, "GET READY! GET SET! GO!" we each stuff fifty ċəlċále
berries into our open mouths & then chew extra fast. sweet tangy juice drips down
our chins. "stick out your tongues!" says Grandpa then he inspects our faces because
he is the judge. "you're all purple!" he says. "no one loses and everyone wins." with
sticky hands and tummies full of berries we race to the creek and take turns diving
in. clear blue ice cold glacier water encircles us as we play tag and swim the day
away catching frogs and tadpoles when the sun disappears into alpine mountains
the sky is the color of flames. everyone returns to camp. "you kids gather kindling
for the fire." our moms and aunties all work together making dinner as us kids
gather firewood. when the fire is ablaze we roast marshmallows and hotdogs.
everyone is storytelling about their adventures and who found the biggest
berries. our languages: nɬeʔkepmxcín, nsyílxcn, and english surround
us as we play. in the morning we wake before the birds and sing
wík'ne ɬ súsəkʷlíʔ! wík'ne ɬ súsəkʷlíʔ! we see the sacred in
everything and the sacred sees us. we are ready
to gather ċəlċále all over again.

ċəlċále	black huckleberries
wík'ne ɬ súsəkʷlíʔ	"I see [jesus] [the Creator]."

Note: I am not sure of the exact translation for "súsəkʷlíʔ" the Elders'
Meadowlark song. The "concept of jesus" would have been introduced
through colonization and Indian Residential Schools, but the word
existed before that. In my interpretation, I visualized the sacred holy
spirit as alive in all things all across tmíxʷ.

frog whisperers

Water
crystal
clear
over
rocks
and
stones.
nothing else exists besides
the creek, the mountain, frogs and tadpoles.
glacier cold on ice cube toes purple lips, purple nose. Mom says, "leave those
"wash your purple cheeks!" berry bucket full: stones, sticks, sand, and water.
mucus soft green frog eggs sway in the stream. tadpoles swim mid-transformation.
us girls wait by the smallest eddy in the creek. STONES must be islands for baby tadpoles
growing little web feet swimming fast all alone. us girls want to bring our baby frogs home
even though Mom says, "STOP!" us girls catch baby frogs anyway. we build their
berry bucket home. "put them frogs back in the creek!" "we love frogs!" we say.
"Grandpa." "yes, Sweetheart," he answers.   "how do you say frog?"
"p̓əp̓éyɬe," he answers.   "Grandpa,
"Grandpa   i will   will i
don't   never   nor   eat
you   eat   knees   a
think   frog's   frog's
frogs are   webbed
Amazing   Toes

Home
a
frogs
"but   our
says, Auntie build
cuzzin, we to
alone!" want
frogs

---

p̓əp̓éyɬe   frog

Educator Connections

Read the editors' thoughts and engage in reflection. Respond to the questions that follow on your own or with your colleague(s).

PERSONAL REFLECTIONS

Christine: I found Nicola Campbell's poems playful and energetic, in sharp contrast to stories of Indigenous trauma. Both poems are written in the voice of a child experiencing the joys of childhood, playing, singing, and interacting with the environment while loving caregivers watch nearby. The poems depict the present times Indigenous families are growing in, fusing both the traditional and the modern—sitting around a fire, roasting marshmallows and hot dogs. They are embraced by a weaving of ancestral ways of being in the world, Indigenous languages as well as English. These poems bring me peace and joy.

Katya: "alpine mountains" shares that "we see the sacred in everything and the sacred sees us." The idea of sacredness rarely enters educational discussions, but so much beauty and love live within this idea. I am amazed at how rigorously playful these poems are, while also carrying sacred stories and memories of ancestral belonging to the land. They are interdisciplinary while also so accessible. I have felt that traditional writing conventions can take a lot of time to teach in classrooms, but this shows what freedom comes when the visual shape and image are given prominence over convention.

EDUCATOR INQUIRY AND ACTIONS

- How do these concrete poems illustrate cultural and land-based teachings?

- As readers, we witness the state of ancestral belonging to the land within these poems. What does that mean to you and how does that make you feel?

- How does the shape challenge or enhance your reading and understanding of each poem's meaning?

- How do you think these poems represent healing?

- What are some ways your school community can provide more opportunities for students to make connections to land-based teachings and experiences? Brainstorm your next steps as a school team.

- In your professional learning community, challenge yourself to create your own concrete poem to represent your understandings of resurgence. Or write two separate poems to represent your understandings of the ideas of truth and reconciliation. This exercise may give you insight into the process and an appreciation of its complexity, as well as a sense of how you might teach this form of writing.

Classroom Connections

Introduce to students the poems and the Connected Concepts you wish to focus on. Use the following questions, prompts, and resource suggestions to guide student learning.

CONNECTED CONCEPTS

- Memories

- Ancestral memory, belonging, and place

- Land-based teachings

CONNECTING TO SELF: PROMPTS FOR PERSONAL REFLECTION

Beginning

- How do these poems make you feel?

- What makes these poems come to life?

Bridging

- Do these poems remind you of a moment or experience in your own life?

- How do you connect with outdoor environments?

- Why do you think Nicola Campbell chose to share her words in this form of poetry?

Beyond

- In what ways is Campbell's writing "creating a narrative of strength, intertwining hearts, minds, and spirits, reminding ourselves of all that is good and strong"?

- How do you think these poems represent healing?

CONNECTING TO COMMUNITY: PROMPTS FOR LEARNING CIRCLES

Beginning

- Share which poem you connected with the most and explain why.

- Share what you noticed or wondered about these poems.

Bridging

- Share a connection you have to these poems.

- Share a fond family memory you have.

Beyond

- Explain where you think Nicola Campbell is from (or describe the place) based on clues from the poems.

- Share your own story, memory, adventure, or experience of being on the land.

Poetry, including the rule-breaking style of concrete poetry (also referred to as visual poetry or shape poetry), is a form of talking back to conventional writing.

- **Problem exposing:** These poems are connected. Try writing two poems that show connections to one concept. This could be used to expose a problem and talk back to it by proposing a solution—for example, colonialism is a problem and Indigenous resurgence is part of the solution of self-determination. Or you could use an image that represents colonialism and an image that represents resurgence to share your thinking and expose the "in-between" space of this issue.

- **Juxtaposing:** Look at these poems alongside a more traditionally formatted text that may not be accessible to a variety of readers (for example, a classroom newsletter or your school's mission statement). Redesign the text in the form of a concrete poem.

INQUIRY

) Beginning

- Bring natural objects inside or, better yet, go outside and spend time in the natural environment. Journal what you see, feel, and wonder. Let these experiences guide the creation of a personal inquiry question—for example, how are clouds formed? What kinds of birds live here?

- Write a concrete poem to represent your understanding of or something you wonder about Orange Shirt Day. Poems could be written in the shape of an orange shirt.

) Bridging

- Explore the question "Where are you from?" Think back to your memories of a particular season to help narrow this inquiry. Think about how you made connections to the land and natural world during this time of year. Check out concrete poem generators online to express your memories and share part of your story digitally.

- Generate a personal or group inquiry question about land-based knowledges as a class—for example, what are traditional medicines that grow in your local area? Ask for the support of Indigenous leaders in your community. Work toward using the mode of concrete poetry to share what you learned.

- Zoom in to a small story (or artifact) in your life that has had a big impact or that carries deep significance for you. Take time to free write. Think about the image that best represents it visually and engage in a process of writing your own concrete poem. Share your poem aloud.

CONNECTIONS TO INDIGENOUS RESOURCES
Books

Mii maanda ezhi-gkendmaanh/This Is How I Know, by Brittany Luby (Groundwood Books, 2021; ages 3–7/grades preK–2).
This dual-language story-poem, written in Anishinaabemowin and English, follows an Anishinaabe child and her grandmother as they explore their environment in each season.

Siha Tooskin Knows the Nature of Life, by Charlene Bearhead and Wilson Bearhead (HighWater Press, 2020; ages 9–11/grades 3–5).
This book shows how Ena Makoochay (Mother Earth) is a teacher, as the main character, an 11-year-old Nakota boy, learns about strength, generosity, kindness, and humility.

The Poet: Pauline Johnson, by David A. Robertson (HighWater Press, 2014; ages 9–11/grades 4–6).
This graphic novel (designed to correspond to grades 4–6 curriculum) is about a shy young girl inspired to overcome her stage fright by the story of Pauline Johnson, a poet of Mohawk descent, who travelled across the continent performing her work in the late 1800s.

Spíləxm: A Weaving of Recovery, Resilience, and Resurgence, by Nicola I. Campbell (HighWater Press, 2021).

Recommended for young adult and adult readers, Nicola Campbell's memoir weaves poetry and prose to tell the story of her life as an intergenerational residential school Survivor. This is a story of healing, resilience, and resurgence.

Online

Rebellion of My Ancestors exhibit, by Jobena Petonoquot. <www.dawsoncollege.qc.ca/art-gallery/exhibitions/jobena-petonoquot-rebellion-of-my-ancestors/>.

In this exhibit, Petonoquot uses an unconventional art approach—found art. Petonoquot's artwork tells the story of her family history as it was affected by colonization in Canada, while showcasing Indigenous resilience.

"Traditions use tools and technology to make the journey easier and more accessible for everyone."

The Paths of Tradition

RUSSELL WALLACE (he/him/his) is an award-winning composer, producer, and traditional singer from the Lil'wat Nation. His music can be heard on soundtracks for film, television, theatre, and dance productions. His most recent album, *Unceded Tongues*, combines Salish musical forms with pop, jazz, and blues, and is sung in the St'át'imc language. Russell is a founding member of the Aboriginal Writers Collective West Coast and an alumnus of the University of British Columbia Creative Writing Program.

TRADITIONS HAVE BEEN around for a long time. Sometimes traditions become static, unlike language, which adapts and changes over time to accommodate new ideas and concepts or the actual changing of how people move their mouths, like how Barcelona became "Barthelona."

Traditions can change too, but they are a little more difficult to change. Sometimes they need to change or they are forced to.

Imagine a village of people: their home represents community, the river that they travel to represents their culture, and the path they use to get to and from the river represents tradition.

Now many years can pass and the same path is used by most of the people because it is the easiest way to access culture and language. Some find other ways that are still close to the easy path used by others, ways that deviate somehow, being easier for those individuals to access for whatever reason. Yet the deviated path reaches the same river.

One day someone notices rocks on the path and clears them away so no one is bothered by the rocks and no one trips or hurts themselves. Another day passes and more rocks are found and again people take the initiative to remove the rocks themselves. Each day there are more rocks and the people begin to talk amongst themselves, and eventually Elders are talked to and stories are shared. You see, there was a rock slide before and the Elders remember from stories from other communities that this can make things difficult for the people. Precautions are taken and people are sent to see what is going on.

If there is no indication anything is wrong, then the community carries on with its daily business.

One night when it is raining hard, the people hear a mighty roar. The people check their community and brace themselves for a big change in the land. As the sun comes up, the people check around the community, venturing in all directions but also being very cautious. Someone comes running and yells that the path to the river is blocked.

The Elders go investigate. The landslide that they feared came overnight and took out a large chunk of the path they used most. At first the people try moving the rocks again, but there are too many and some are too big. (A side note: Rock slides are to be avoided by the St'át'imc people because of the illnesses that are associated with such things. Rodent droppings in the rocks become exposed and serious illnesses can infect and devastate a small community.)

The people need access to the river, so some of the more able-bodied people go to find another path. It takes some time and a lot of bruised knees and twisted ankles, but some new paths are carved in the fallen rocks.

Eventually the whole village is able to access the river again, although the paths are different. Some people maintain a diligent and faithful adherence to the old path no matter how difficult it is. Others create new paths and allow only their families to access them. Others deviate again and find a way they can access the river that is best for them.

Colonialism has obscured and covered up many things from our past and yet we have languages and cultures that still thrive. Five hundred years of genocidal tendencies, though, have made an impact on our histories, language, culture, arts, bloodlines, food securities, and lands. Epidemics have devastated communities. Lack of access to traditional diets and the poisoning of the lands and waters have led to health issues. A lot of these assaults on our culture and language have come swiftly and violently. Some of these assaults have crept up slowly, almost imperceptibly, until it was too late. Some of our traditions changed out of necessity.

For this journey on the path to culture, we also need a map and a walking stick, which are considered tools, and we need good safe shoes or a vehicle, which are considered technology. Traditions use tools and technology to make the journey easier and more accessible for everyone.

The river is still there, but sometimes even that changes its course due to cataclysms of the earth; the community of people is still there, but the path they have learned to use to access the river has changed drastically for some. Some people have left the community altogether, but sometimes they come back and need to access that river again.

That river is my culture and songs. That community is my family and ancestors, and the path they taught me may differ from others in the community. The path that my mother taught me to access is there because she encouraged me to share this path so that others may access the river. But, then again, others may find their own way that is best for them.

Nothing can remain static, not even the earth upon which we walk. Our languages, our cultures, our traditions change and adapt. Language, culture, and tradition keep us alive so that we can transmit them to others and to future generations.

Educator Connections

Read the editors' thoughts and engage in reflection. Respond to the questions that follow on your own or with your colleague(s).

PERSONAL REFLECTIONS

Christine: I appreciate Russell Wallace using this story as a metaphor for culture. I am reminded of the resiliency of my culture, and how my ancestors had to constantly adapt and change with the times in order for our culture and traditions to survive. Unfortunately, in my family, part of adapting was dissociating from culture to better fit into settler society, so for us, a lot (but not all) of our family's cultural knowledge has been lost. I'm thankful to those who have made connecting to culture more accessible for youth, as I owe a lot of my cultural knowledge to the families and organizations working to ensure it continues to be passed down.

Katya: I feel a need to acknowledge my privilege of having many traditions that were nurtured and preserved rather than forced to adapt and change in order to survive. This piece reminds me of the importance of continuing cultural traditions for my children and the next generations, while also supporting Indigenous cultural reclamations and working to expose the colonial structures that threatened the traditions in the first place. I feel that I need to acknowledge this great privilege. This essay makes me wonder if paths of tradition could have crossed without disruption.

EDUCATOR INQUIRY AND ACTIONS

- As a school community, in what ways do you provide paths for students to access their cultures and languages? Consider how you might use tools and technology to support new paths forward.

- Consider some of the traditions at your school. Who are they for and do they reflect what your community currently values? Consider using this frame: Which school-based traditions could stop, which should continue, and what might be new paths forward? For example, you could start with something easy such as whether or not students are allowed to chew gum at school and bridge into more challenging topics such as standing for "O Canada."

- Discuss the metaphor of taking "different paths to the same river"? How might this metaphor also relate to classroom teaching, learning, and curriculum?

- Russell Wallace lists many ways that colonialism has made "assaults on our culture and language." Review this list as a group and inquire deeper into one of these. Share your learning with your colleagues.

- What are some teacher moves you can make to encourage students to think metaphorically?

- This text presents similar ideas to those put forth by the Truth and Reconciliation Commission but does so differently; the TRC uses testimony and facts, and Russell Wallace uses metaphor. Think about the lessons you are learning from responding to the truth aspect of the TRC. Challenge yourself to frame your learning (or unlearning) through a metaphor. How might you represent the work you plan to continue?

Classroom Connections

Introduce to students the narrative and the Connected Concepts you wish to focus on. Use the following questions, prompts, and resource suggestions to guide student learning.

CONNECTED CONCEPTS

- Traditions

- Fluidity of culture

- Learning through metaphor

CONNECTING TO SELF: PROMPTS FOR PERSONAL REFLECTION

Beginning
- What are some of your family traditions?

- What have you learned from a story?

Bridging
- How do you contribute to keeping traditions alive?

- How do cultures change over time?

Beyond
- In your experience, how have tools, technology, or strategies supported the preservation of traditions?

- Has colonization threatened your culture? If so, how?

CONNECTING TO COMMUNITY: PROMPTS FOR LEARNING CIRCLES

) Beginning

- Share one of your family's traditions.

- Share a lesson you learned through a story.

) Bridging

- Share a story about how you overcame or adapted to a challenge.

- Share a metaphor for the role of culture in your life.

● Beyond

- Share your own pathways and journeys to traditions. Consider your experience preserving, reconnecting to, or reclaiming traditions.

- Discuss the importance of culture, including what our cultures teach us.

TALKING BACK

It is important to acknowledge that efforts to preserve colonial traditions and ways of doing things in Canada have blocked Indigenous paths to culture. How can culture and traditions be beneficial and how can they be harmful?

- **Problem exposing:** This piece exposes the effects of colonization and attempted genocide on individuals and communities. Within this context, surviving itself is talking back. What are some "Canadian" traditions that should be or are being questioned? Connect to the story of how First Nations student Skyla Hart talked back to the tradition of standing for "O Canada."[1]

---

1   See Jill Coubrough, "First Nations Student Reprimanded After Not Standing for O Canada," CBC News, September 22, 2021, www.cbc.ca/news/canada/manitoba /winnipeg-student-reprimanded-o-canada-wfpcbc-cbc-1.6179258.

- **Juxtaposing:** Juxtapose Russell Wallace's narrative with an example of Indigenous futurism. Indigenous futurism is a growing artistic movement where Indigenous writers imagine alternative histories and futures through the exploration of science fiction. What can Indigenous futurism teach us about the dynamic nature of Indigenous culture and its ability to transcend time?

INQUIRY

Beginning

- Why is language an important part of culture? Learn from a local Indigenous Elder or Knowledge Keeper and write a paragraph summarizing your learning.

Bridging

- How have paths to culture and language been blocked for Indigenous people? Are there contemporary and ongoing examples of this? Find a video of an Indigenous person discussing this and present it to your classmates.

- Sketch your own paths to tradition. Using Russell Wallace's narrative as inspiration, draw your own river, village, and rocks to tell about your journey. Or create a metaphor to describe your experiences. How have your family or community traditions changed? Adapted? Been reclaimed? This will take time; it is not about a finished product, but rather to encourage you to engage with the Connected Concepts.

Beyond

- What Indigenous languages in Canada are on the brink of extinction? What Indigenous languages are thriving? Develop a presentation to showcase your research results.

- What are some language revitalization efforts happening in Canada? What are some language revitalization efforts happening around the world? Find an example of how technology is being used in language revitalization efforts and explain it to the class.

- Did Canada commit genocide? Explore the United Nations' definition of genocide and write an essay comparing it to the Canadian government's treatment of Indigenous communities throughout history.[2]

CONNECTIONS TO INDIGENOUS RESOURCES

Book

"kitaskinaw 2350," by Chelsea Vowel, from *This Place: 150 Years Retold* (HighWater Press, 2019; ages 15–18/grades 9–12).
This story, an example of Indigenous futurism in graphic novel form, envisions a future shaped by Indigenous people. The story takes place in the year 2350 and follows a young Cree woman as she time-travels back to 2012, viewing that time through the lens of the future.

Magazine

"Issue 10: Matriarchy," *Red Rising Magazine*. <redrising.ca>.
This issue of the Indigenous-run grassroots organization's annual magazine explores the concept of matriarchy as a way of life that has been held by many Indigenous communities for millennia.

Online

Metis In Space podcast, by Chelsea Vowel and Molly Swain (2014–).
In their podcast, Vowel and Swain deconstruct the science-fiction genre through a decolonial lens, reviewing movies and television shows featuring Indigenous peoples and themes.

---

2   Available at <www.un.org/en/genocideprevention/genocide.shtml>.

Making a Comeback
as an Artist

VICTORIA MCINTOSH, also known as Biktoryias, has a strong bond to stories and identifies as ikwe (woman, water carrier). Transitioning from artist to educator, she now merges both gifts into sharing what she sees in her life. Working with many different mediums and combining traditional storytelling with artworks, she strives to create deeper meaning and understanding of Indigenous teachings.

———

IT HAS BEEN a long road with many lessons along the way as I think of my time with my family on the North Shore of Sagkeeng. I was lonely and craved attention as a child, and creativity helped me fill these emotions as I watched my grandmother draw and sew. I remember the small lantern she would place by her side by the window as it started getting dark. She would always go by the lightness and darkness of the day to get ready for the next day. At this time, there was no running water or electricity that we could rely on, and when I think back, I am amazed at her resiliency to keep moving forward with whatever she had on hand. Her favourite art forms were sewing and quilting.

When my own mother was tragically killed in 2016, it left a large gap within my spirit; to lose someone so suddenly can make us question many beliefs that we follow. As I unwrapped all the quilt patches my mother had, I noticed one particular bag. Just like her mother, my grandmother, she would put away certain items that had significant meanings. When I looked into the bag, I was delighted to see the flour sacks my mother had saved all this time. The memories flooded in. These findings revealed that sewing

"By reconnecting with the ways

of our people through artwork,

we can reconcile first with ourselves

by reclaiming our identities through

our creations and stories."

and upcycling were essential for our community—nothing went to waste, anything that could be was given back to the earth. Everything came in cycles, the circles of all the stories and learnings our grandmother shared with us as we listened to her.

I realized then that quilting or sewing was not just about the act itself, but was a self-chosen activity for well-being. We can say that quilting is influenced by the emotional state of the quilter. As I held up the materials, I knew I needed to continue on to tell the stories of the women in my family.

By reconnecting with the ways of our people through artwork, we can reconcile first with ourselves by reclaiming our identities through our creations and stories. As a Survivor, *Let the Children Play* is my legacy and appreciation to the Creator that I'm still here and have work to do, while some have travelled to the spirit world. Many in my family were taken to residential school, including myself, and the painting describes reconnecting with family traditions, with my language, and with the stories that were told to me by my grandmother, who did not speak English. The stories had deeper spiritual meaning for us, but we were told by the nuns and priests that all these stories were heathen, pagan, and fairy tales of the devil.

As an Anishinaabe artist and storyteller, my creations are my way of reconnecting with the gifts given to me by Kitchi-Manitou (the mysterious one). As artists, we are given the role of dream keepers and translators to help others who may be struggling with something in their everyday lives.

Let the Children Play, by Victoria McIntosh.

(Image courtesy of Victoria McIntosh.)

Educator Connections

Read the editors' thoughts and engage in reflection. Respond to the questions that follow on your own or with your colleague(s).

PERSONAL REFLECTIONS

Christine: Victoria McIntosh's painting and accompanying narrative expose the healing power of art. For many people, art is a coping mechanism that has the potential to illuminate hidden aspects of the self, leading to a deeper sense of identity. Through her artwork, Victoria McIntosh is reconnecting with her ancestors and her inner child, commanding "Let the children play."

Katya: I can hear Victoria McIntosh's voice in this work. I had an opportunity as a university student to listen to her share her residential school story. When I read this work, I can vividly remember an outfit her mother made for her that she shared with everyone. I remember the woolly texture of the jacket and the cold buttons. When I read McIntosh's words and take in her beautiful artwork I am inspired to do better as a teacher. I really think that joy and play must be part of the solution.

EDUCATOR INQUIRY AND ACTIONS

- As a teacher, how do you create an environment that fosters joy and play in a way that is empowering for young people?

- How are the arts part of reconnecting to culture and identity for students?

- Consider your plans as a school team or grade group. What is the role of creativity in your school or learning community? What is the role of well-being? If these are not prominent, how might you revise your plans to ensure they are incorporated?

- Consider how you might use Victoria McIntosh's reflection on "making a comeback as an artist" when discussing the National Day for Truth and Reconciliation or responding to the Truth and Reconciliation Commission's Calls to Action. Share your plans with colleagues.

Classroom Connections

Introduce to students the narrative and artwork and the Connected Concepts you wish to focus on. Use the following questions, prompts, and resource suggestions to guide student learning.

CONNECTED CONCEPTS

- Indigenous art/creations

- Role of play and joy in learning

- Intergenerational stories

CONNECTING TO SELF: PROMPTS FOR PERSONAL REFLECTION

❭ Beginning

- What do you like to do for fun?

- What brings you joy?

❭ Bridging

- What story topics are your favourite?

- What have you learned from observing others? What have you learned from stories?

● Beyond

- Think about playful experiences you had when you were a young child. How do you think these experiences brought you a sense of well-being?

- What artistic elements does Victoria McIntosh use in her painting? How do these elements add meaning to her piece?

CONNECTING TO COMMUNITY: PROMPTS FOR LEARNING CIRCLES

Beginning

- Share your favourite story from childhood.

- Share a story that has been shared through generations of your family or community.

Bridging

- Share a comeback story.

- Share what choice you would make if you could have dinner with any person in the history of the world, dead or alive, and explain why you would choose this person.

Beyond

- Share an art piece by an Indigenous artist and discuss why and how you connected to this piece.

- Describe an intergenerational story or tradition from your life that lives on through sharing.

TALKING BACK

Victoria McIntosh's art talks back to her residential school experience and is a reclamation of her identity and culture. *Let the Children Play* is a depiction of children playing, which is a child's right, according to the United Nations Convention on the Rights of the Child.[1]

---

1   Available on the website of the United Nations Office of the High Commissioner for Human Rights: <www.ohchr.org/en/professionalinterest/pages/crc.asp>.

- **Problem exposing:** This piece exposes the damaging psychological effects of residential schools on children; within this context, joy and play is talking back to that. Victoria McIntosh explains that her painting "describes reconnecting with family traditions, with my language, and with the stories that were told to me by my grandmother... The stories had deeper spiritual meaning for us, but we were told by the nuns and priests that all these stories were heathen, pagan, and fairy tales of the devil." What is her rebuttal to the ignorant beliefs of the nuns and priests? What role do artists play in Indigenous communities?

- **Juxtaposing:** Look at the images in the exhibit entitled *There Is Truth Here: Creativity and Resilience in Children's Art from Indian Residential and Day Schools.*[2] Compare and contrast these pieces (for example, their imagery and colours) with Victoria McIntosh's *Let the Children Play.*

INQUIRY

⟩ Beginning

- How can you share your favourite story from childhood in a format other than a verbal telling? Pick one format and recreate your story to share with the class.

- Map all the ways you play in your life. Or create a timeline to show different ways you have played since you were little, and reflect on what has changed and what has stayed the same.

⟩ Bridging

- How can you create upcycled art that tells a particular story about something? Pick a story you want to tell and create something!

- How can stories be passed down through generations? Find an example of a story that has been passed down and share it with the class.

---

2   University of Victoria, Legacy Art Galleries, legacy.uvic.ca/gallery/truth/.

- Research another prominent Indigenous artist (for example, Norval Morrisseau or Daphne Odjig) who uses painting as a medium and describe their contribution to Indigenous art.

- **Beyond**
  - How can art be used for activism? Find an example and describe the context and the art to the class.

  - How have other historically oppressed groups engaged in reconnecting with their culture and identity? Present your findings to the class in the format of your choice.

  - What are the rights of a child? Look up UNICEF's child-friendly version of the Convention on the Rights of the Child.[3] Create an infographic to share your learning about a right you think needs more attention and show how your school community can take action.

CONNECTIONS TO INDIGENOUS RESOURCES

Books
My Heart Fills With Happiness, by Monique Gray Smith (Orca Books, 2016; ages 1–5/grades preK–K).
This board book, written to support the wellness of Indigenous children and their families, asks young readers to think about what makes them happy, celebrating the moments that bring them joy. (Also available in French: *J'ai le coeur rempli de bonheur.*)

We All Play, by Julie Flett (Greystone Kids, 2021; ages 1–7/grades preK–2). Featuring Cree and English, this story encapsulates the joy of play, focusing on both children and animals in nature.

---

3   Available at <www.unicef.org/sop/convention-rights-child-child-friendly-version>.

Sk̲'ad'a Stories series, by Sara Florence Davidson and Robert Davidson (HighWater Press, 2021–2022; ages 6–8/grades 1–3).
The books in this series connect to the theme of intergenerational stories, focusing on learning through observation and the role of Elders in sharing knowledge and mentorship.

The Gift Is in the Making, by Leanne Betasamosake Simpson (HighWater Press, 2013; ages 9–11/grades 4–6).
This book retells previously published Anishinaabeg stories that celebrate diversity, gentleness, and humour. The stories were originally collected by the author to share with her children as a way to connect to their culture and nation.

Online
"It's 'Time to Play' at WAG as It Unveils Sculpture by Inuit Artist," Radio Canada, February 8, 2021. <www.rcinet.ca/en/2021/02/08/its-time-to-play -at-wag-as-it-unveils-sculpture-by-inuit-artist>.
This article and video highlight Inuk artist Abraham Anghik Ruben's sculpture of a mother bear and her cubs, which speaks to the importance of love, safety, and play.

We Are Inherently Mathematical

CHRISTINA LAVALLEY RUDDY, a member of Algonquins of Pikwakanagan First Nation, is an artist, researcher, mentor, and advocate. She has spent her career working to empower Indigenous youth through education, language, and capacity building, in settings such as friendship centres and post-secondary institutions. In 2018, Christina received Lakehead University's Indigenous Partnership Research Award, with Dr. Ruth Beatty, in recognition of her leadership in incorporating Indigenous knowledge into the Ontario mathematics curriculum.

———

A S A FIRST Nations artist, I always considered art to be my hobby. It relaxes me, and it gives me peace and an extreme amount of pleasure to gift what I can to family and friends, and not just for special occasions. It is commonly known that if you come to my home and there is new beadwork or art that you see and like, it's yours.

When I was very young, I was blessed with a step-grandmother from my First Nation who took me to small classes at a community member's kitchen table, where we made moccasins and purses and so many things. After that, life took off in a different direction and I struggled with my identity and where I fit in the world, as people tend to in their teens and early twenties.

When I started working at a college as an event planner with the Indigenous Studies department, I had the opportunity to revisit crafting, beading, and leatherwork. I knew from that experience that working with leather was not something I enjoyed, although I feel privileged to have spent time with people who do. They taught me about the chrome side, the grain, and how

"What I saw in that classroom is something I only dreamed of when I was young—that I could be myself in every space I was in."

to cut leather properly, and now I get to share that knowledge with others. When I discovered loom beading, I first taught myself by watching some videos; then, by sharing my enthusiasm for it, I discovered so many others who taught me their tricks and encouraged me to play more and create my own way of practising the skill of looming. On top of looming, I found amazing students who would bring their beads to school and teach me and others multiple stitches and types of beading. There I was again, at a table surrounded by others who were sharing their gifts, telling stories, and sharing who they were as Indigenous people.

LEFT: An example of loom beading in progress.
(Image courtesy of Christina Lavalley Ruddy.)

RIGHT: An example of a finished bracelet, created on a bead loom.
(Image courtesy of Christina Lavalley Ruddy.)

In 2012, I received a request from a group of academics who were studying how First Nations people may have learned math pre-contact. They wanted to see what loom beading was. I was nervous and curious, but I say yes to pretty much everything, so I saw no harm in a bunch of academics coming to see me play and bead. When their eyes lit up, I didn't understand what they saw. *I am Native, I can't do math*, I thought, and I knew this because I had spent most of my career being told that, as a Native person, I couldn't. But they saw something I didn't, and when they asked me to come to a grade 6 math class to teach students to loom bead, I thought it was no big deal; I was just going along for the ride.

Going back to my former elementary school was harder than I thought it would be. I was one of the first Indigenous students at the school, and visiting those hallways again was like time-travelling back to being that little girl who was bullied and abused by peers and sometimes even teachers. It was scary and took my breath away. I was lucky enough to be accompanied through the school by a teacher who was caring and kind and didn't question when I needed time to recover before entering the classroom.

In a past job, I would tell young people who were considering what career path to choose to find what comes easily and brings them happiness; if they could do that it would never feel like "work." What happened in the classroom from that day forward changed me to the core of my being as a First Nations person and taught me what it truly means to love what I do every day.

Over the next few weeks, the teacher and I worked together to teach the students; he took the math parts and I did the beading parts. We found a rhythm that worked for us and had fun learning from the students as they discovered the math in their beautiful patterns and creations. But something else was happening too. Again, I was sitting at a table of students learning together, teaching, sharing, and laughing. This was research, this was math, and this was school—it's not supposed to be that way, right? I didn't know sharing my love of beads with students could be so fulfilling.

I watched the students, both the Indigenous students and their non-Indigenous peers, embrace the culture. They had conversations about powwow, community, regalia, family—we created a safe space for that to happen. We created a space where Indigenous students were safe to share who they are and their way of life where those conversations had not

Grade 8 students, taught by the author, work on their own
loom beading projects.

(Image courtesy of Christina Lavalley Ruddy.)

happened before. Growing up Indigenous sometimes means you have your home identity and your school and work identity. What I saw in that classroom is something I only dreamed of when I was young—that I could be myself in every space I was in.

Beyond the incredible student learning, I was slowly learning, day by day, that as Indigenous people we are inherently mathematical. Witnessing students who would freeze and even tear up at the thought of switching to math class suddenly stand at the front of the class debating their peers about algebra was incredible. Watching a young girl get frustrated, walk away to take a break, and come back to the task instead of crying tears of frustration and building a wall around herself in seconds that would never be torn down was inspiring and breathtaking.

After four years of doing this work, I stood making a presentation to a very intimidating group of senior educators. I described our work, and for the first time in over 40 years spoke out loud the words "I can do math." This breakthrough, this moment, has become my new foundation, has given me the strength that drives me and the bravery to tear down every barrier, stereotype, and glass ceiling that stands in my way.

We can do math. We are inherently mathematical.

Educator Connections

Read the editors' thoughts and engage in reflection. Respond to the questions that follow on your own or with your colleague(s).

PERSONAL REFLECTIONS

Christine: Christina Lavalley Ruddy's essay captures everything I love about my profession. It reminds me of when I was a student teacher and I started a beading club at lunch at the junior high where I was completing my practicum. Many of the Indigenous students there were disconnected from their culture, and beading was their first act of reconnecting. We spent many lunch hours eating, talking, and beading, and I tried my best to pass on a few teachings about beading that I had learned. To this day, that experience of having the honour to teach them a snippet of their culture and seeing their eyes light up with pride at how beautiful their creations turned out is a major highlight of my career.

Katya: Christina Lavalley Ruddy's words and beadwork help to make the idea of resurgence visible and concrete. Her story of her negative school experiences and bravely bringing her First Nations cultural practices to life in classrooms in a way that inspires future generations is a beautiful and powerful example of resurgence. I can see how loom beading teachings help make so many connections between culture, intergenerational stories, history, and geography. At the beginning of the pandemic, I had the opportunity to connect with Christina, and her work has inspired a collaborative teacher inquiry at my school into how math and culture are already woven together. Like the beads on a loom, it is something that is bringing our unique stories and experiences together with so many learning possibilities!

EDUCATOR INQUIRY AND ACTIONS

- What does Christina Lavalley Ruddy share that indicates that loom beading is more than just a craft?

- Individually and as a school team, reflect on your beliefs about and school experiences of teaching mathematics. Do you see your identity reflected in the content or processes?

- Look at the images presented here. What math and curricular connections are inherently woven into loom beading? Brainstorm curricular connections and possibilities.

- What is *ethnomathematics* and how might this area of study be helpful to your school or professional learning community?[1] Reflect on how building your knowledge of this idea may also support student learning in mathematics and instill a sense of cultural pride.

- What are you currently doing as a teacher to make learning in mathematics joyful and supportive of cultural knowledges?

- How can you create a sense of community within the classroom that honours culture and risk-taking?

- Christina Lavalley Ruddy shares the experience of co-teaching that brought beading and math together. Share a story of a teaching collaboration where you and a colleague "found a rhythm" and taught together in a way that was fulfilling to you and your students.

- What are Indigenous beading practices in your local area? If you were to inquire into one of these, how would you do this in a culturally responsive and respectful way? Think about how to involve Indigenous Knowledge Keepers and community partnerships.[2]

- How can you ensure that your school is not engaging in cultural appropriation, but rather cultural appreciation? Share some best practices that you know of, such as not jumping into this work without proper consultation with Indigenous experts.

---

1   See Ubiratan D'Ambrosio, "Ethnomathematics and Its Place in the History and Pedagogy of Mathematics," *For the Learning of Mathematics* 5, no. 1 (1985): 44–48.

2   See, for example, Ruth Beatty and Colinda Clyne, "Relationships and Reciprocity Towards Decolonizing Mathematics Education," *Journal of Higher Education Theory and Practice* 20, no. 7 (2020): 122–127.

Classroom Connections

Introduce to students the narrative and images and the Connected Concepts you wish to focus on. Use the following questions, prompts, and resource suggestions to guide student learning.

CONNECTED CONCEPTS

- Beading

- Ethnomathematics

- Cultural appropriation

- Cultural pride

CONNECTING TO SELF: PROMPTS FOR PERSONAL REFLECTION

) **Beginning**

- What is your favourite thing to make? What about this process brings you joy?

- If you could learn to make anything in the world, what would it be and why?

- Who is your favourite person to learn from? What makes them a great teacher?

) **Bridging**

- Look at the images of beadwork. What do you see? What do you notice?

- Have you ever struggled with where you "fit in the world"? What helped you deal with this?

- Have you ever taken a class outside of school (for example, a cooking or language class)? What did you learn about?

● **Beyond**

- Reflect on your beliefs about and experiences of learning math in and out of school. Is it something you enjoy? Why or why not?

- What is an example of cultural appropriation? Why do you think it's harmful?

- Think about something you do in your everyday life that involves mathematics. What mathematics are involved in that activity?

CONNECTING TO COMMUNITY: PROMPTS FOR LEARNING CIRCLES

Beginning

- Share an artifact or heirloom that instills a sense of cultural pride.

- Discuss a time when you learned a skill from someone. Describe what skill you learned, who taught you, and how learning that skill made you feel.

- Share a hobby that relaxes you and brings you peace.

Bridging

- Share the story or significance of a cultural artifact that involved a form of mathematics in its creation.

- Describe a time when you collaborated with someone and "found a rhythm," and when learning together was good for your head and your heart.

- Christina Lavalley Ruddy encourages students to "find what comes easily and brings them happiness." Share what you would love to spend your days doing.

Beyond

- Christina Lavalley Ruddy remembers thinking, "I can't do math." Share a limiting belief you currently carry and transform it into an "I can" statement.

- Think about if your home identity is different from your school identity, or if you can be yourself in any space, like Christina Lavalley Ruddy. Explain.

- Share a story about a time when you had the strength and bravery to tear down a "barrier, stereotype, [or] glass ceiling" that stood in your way.

Ethnomathematics melds culture and mathematics and talks back to the Eurocentric nature of many current curricular documents.[3] While STEAM (science, technology, engineering, arts, and mathematics) is a current educational buzzword, consider how Indigenous pedagogies have always inherently incorporated elements of STEAM.

- **Problem exposing:** Christina Lavalley Ruddy exposes the feeling that she could not do math and her traumatic experiences of being bullied and abused by both peers and teachers. Think about your math identity. What positive and negative experiences have you had in relation to math?

  Look at beading through different lenses (for example, historical, geographical, or political) to reveal some of the tensions around this cultural practice. How has colonization challenged or changed beading practices? How has beading become a source of resurgence?

- **Juxtaposing:** Find an image or text that provides an example of cultural appropriation and juxtapose this with an example of cultural appreciation. Compare and contrast these texts and discuss your noticings and why these are relevant to the topics of resurgence and cultural pride.

INQUIRY

⟩ Beginning

- Learn about the Indigenous cultural creations made in your area. What materials are used to make them? How are these artifacts expressions of cultural pride?

- Create a slideshow showcasing beautiful examples of cultural creations from a variety of nations. What nations is each creation specific to? How are creations across the continent similar to and different from each other?

---

3   See D'Ambrosio, "Ethnomathematics and Its Place in the History and Pedagogy of Mathematics," 44–48.

- Find a story about an Indigenous cultural creation. What does the story teach you?

- Learn from an Indigenous artist about the beading techniques and teachings in your area. What values do the teachings instill?

- Use a process of backwards design to look at the beadwork images presented here and guide a math talk. How are they "inherently mathematical"? Look at all the different math topics and ideas that come from this example. You could then try this with another cultural creation and see if there are connections between the two.

- Why is it necessary to learn about Indigenous cultural creations from Indigenous peoples? Explore the concept of cultural appropriation. What is the difference between cultural appropriation and cultural appreciation?

● **Beyond**

- Explore the mathematics involved in the making of an Indigenous cultural creation (such as beading, birch bark basket making, or canoe building) specific to your region. What mathematical concepts are used?

- What is ethnomathematics? Research this concept and create a presentation to share your learning.

- How are Indigenous groups around the world working to make cultural appropriation illegal? Research the legalities around cultural appropriation and how delegates from the United Nations are working to combat Indigenous appropriation worldwide.

CONNECTIONS TO INDIGENOUS RESOURCES

Books

Powwow Counting in Cree, by Penny M. Thomas (HighWater Press, 2013; ages 3–5/grades preK–K).

This book for early years readers (or older readers who would like to learn how to count in Cree) could be used to support the integration of the Cree language into math.

One Drum: Stories and Ceremonies for a Planet, by Richard Wagamese (Douglas & McIntyre, 2019).

This collection of stories and ceremonies rooted in the Anishinaabe way of life guides readers in the seven sacred teachings of love, respect, humility, courage, wisdom, truth, and honesty.

Online

"Decolonizing Math Education: What We Can Learn From Indigenous Teaching Methods," Social Sciences and Humanities Research Council (2021). <www.sshrc-crsh.gc.ca/society-societe/stories-histoires/story-histoire -eng.aspx?story_id=316&utm_source=sshrc_homepagE&Utm_medium =websitE&Utm_campaign=Rsid_316_EN>.

This article describes the research project that Christina Lavalley Ruddy references in her essay. It also provides additional links and resources to understand more about the project.

Math Catcher Outreach Program, Simon Fraser University. <www.sfu.ca /mathcatcher.html>.

This outreach program uses First Nations imagery and storytelling to introduce math and science to students. The program teaches how math is used in everyday life and forms the basis for many of our daily decisions and lifelong choices.

THE
FOOTBRIDGE
SERIES

)) ◗ ● ●

THE FOOTBRIDGE SERIES aims to bridge curricular outcomes with Indigenous-centred content and perspectives from a range of nations and places. Like a footbridge, this series provides a path between Indigenous worldviews and the classroom, engaging differences, including tensions, and highlighting the importance of balance, all while helping teachers integrate Indigenous perspectives into their own learning and multiple disciplines within K–12 education and beyond.